THE
Trusted
TEACHER

A Reflective Guide for
Impactful Relationships
With Secondary Students

ERICA
BATTLE

Solution Tree | Press

a division of
Solution Tree

555 North Morton Street
Bloomington, IN 47404
800.733.6786 (toll free) / 812.336.7700
FAX: 812.336.7790

email: info@SolutionTree.com
SolutionTree.com
Visit go.SolutionTree.com/SEL to download the free reproducibles in this book.

Printed in the United States of America

Library of Congress Cataloging-in-Publication Data

Names: Battle, Erica, author.
Title: The trusted teacher : a reflective guide for impactful relationships
   with secondary students / Erica Battle.
Description: Bloomington, IN : Solution Tree Press, [2024] | Includes
   bibliographical references and index.
Identifiers: LCCN 2024016234 (print) | LCCN 2024016235 (ebook) | ISBN
   9781960574626 (paperback) | ISBN 9781960574633 (ebook)
Subjects: LCSH: Affective education. | Social learning. | Academic
   achievement.
Classification: LCC LB1072 .B38 2024 (print) | LCC LB1072 (ebook) | DDC
   370.15/34--dc23/eng20240823
LC record available at https://lccn.loc.gov/2024016234
LC ebook record available at https://lccn.loc.gov/2024016235

Solution Tree
Jeffrey C. Jones, CEO
Edmund M. Ackerman, President

Solution Tree Press
President and Publisher: Douglas M. Rife
Associate Publishers: Todd Brakke and Kendra Slayton
Editorial Director: Laurel Hecker
Art Director: Rian Anderson
Copy Chief: Jessi Finn
Production Editor: Madonna Evans
Proofreader: Elijah Oates
Text and Cover Designer: Julie Csizmadia
Acquisitions Editors: Carol Collins and Hilary Goff
Content Development Specialist: Amy Rubenstein
Associate Editors: Sarah Ludwig and Elijah Oates
Editorial Assistant: Anne Marie Watkins

Acknowledgments

Writing a professional resource to support thousands of teachers, who in turn will impact countless students, is an immensely challenging yet rewarding task. I'm deeply grateful to Solution Tree for providing me with the opportunity to share my insights and thoughts on the crucial topic of adolescent social-emotional wellness.

A heartfelt thank you to the most patient and inspiring editor an author could ever wish for, Hilary Goff. You were truly a blessing throughout this journey. Your challenges to my approach and thinking were invaluable, helping me to craft a resource that empowers secondary school teachers to reflect on their practice and better meet their students' needs.

Immense gratitude goes out to the educators who acted as my sounding board. Your feedback on each chapter was pivotal, helping me navigate and refine my thoughts and ideas. Also thank you very much to the teachers who contributed to this book by allowing me to interview them.

Finally, I must extend my deepest thanks to every student I've had the privilege of teaching. It is your influence that enables me to create this work. Our interactions have profoundly shaped the educator I am today, and for that, I am eternally thankful to each one of you.

To my husband Barrett, whenever I felt unsure, you were right there cheering me on. You have been my biggest supporter and cheerleader since day one, and I'm happy to share this accomplishment with you. You pushed my thinking and helped me talk through ideas, and for that, I thank you!

To my children, Darrius, Micah, and Maxwell, you all inspire me to dream bigger. I appreciate you all hyping me up when you see my accomplishments and ensuring to shout me out on your social media pages! It does my heart well to see I make you proud.

To my Momma and Sister Michelle, you two are officially cheerleaders five and six. You have been sources of encouragement when I felt like I had no more words to write. You continued to push me to keep going while providing much-needed support. I thank you both for encouraging me to strive for greatness in all I do. I truly appreciate you.

Solution Tree Press would like to thank the following reviewers:

Lauren Aragon
Instructional Specialist for
    Innovation & Development
Pasadena Independent
    School District
Houston, Texas

Doug Crowley
Assistant Principal
DeForest Area High School
DeForest, Wisconsin

Nicholas Emmanuele
High School English Teacher and
    Department Chair
McDowell Intermediate High
    School
Erie, Pennsylvania

Jennifer Renegar
Data & Assessment Specialist
Republic School District
Republic, Missouri

Justin Schafer
Assistant Principal
Flint Springs Elementary School
Huntington, Indiana

A REFLECTIVE GUIDE FOR
IMPACTFUL RELATIONSHIPS
WITH SECONDARY STUDENTS

Visit **go.SolutionTree.com/SEL** to download
the free reproducibles in this book.

Table of Contents

Reproducibles are in italics

About the Author

Erica Battle, an Educational Consultant with Life Changes in Progress Educational Consulting, has worked with thousands of educators across the United States, providing professional development and coaching support. Throughout her years in education, Erica has held various roles, such as classroom teacher, instructional specialist, teacher mentor, and Director of RTI with a focus on literacy. Erica's knowledge encompasses a broad range of educational topics, such as social-emotional wellness, effective literacy practices, instructional practices that yield results, data-driven instruction, and instructional leadership. Erica has had the privilege of supporting leaders, teachers, and students in urban, rural, and suburban communities throughout the United States and the U.S. Virgin Islands.

In addition to her consulting work, Erica is also a published author. She wrote and published an adolescent self-discovery book titled *Who Are You? A Guide to Help Adolescents Navigate Through the Social and Emotional Issues of Life*. This program is used by middle schools, high schools, and organizations around the United States. Erica has also released her reading comprehension resource, *A. R. E. You Actively Reading and Engaging*™ Reading Comprehension System. This supplemental resource supports intentional and explicit instruction in reading comprehension for grade 3 through college.

Erica received her BS from Tennessee State University and her MAT from Trevecca Nazarene University, and she completed her educational leadership coursework from Lipscomb University.

Introduction

My first year of teaching was a catalyst for my education career. I had no plans to become a teacher. To be honest, I started teaching because I had lost a job and needed to support my family, and it just made sense at the time. But something happened over the course of that year. I had a classroom full of smart students who very seldom received a chance due to their socioeconomic status, where they lived, and past behavior. I realized I could help these students appreciate that their lives were much bigger than their current circumstances and they could accomplish anything they set their minds to. It was that year I realized I was meant to be a teacher.

As a student, I had a complicated relationship with school, and this was likely why teaching didn't call to me initially. Prior to middle school, school had been my happy place. But beginning in eighth grade, I struggled with major issues in my home life, and school started to feel like an unsafe place for me.

This ultimately led to me not graduating from high school on time. I dreaded going to school. I didn't feel a sense of belonging with my peers or with the teachers I saw each day. I skipped assignments and began acting out. My eighth-grade principal vowed to keep me off the cheerleading squad and ensured that I didn't get to go on any school-sponsored trips. She made sure my final year in middle school was memorable, and not in a loving, fuzzy-feeling type of way (Battle, 2020). It was then I made up my mind that school didn't matter, and neither did I.

What I didn't realize as a child was that I was traumatized by what I experienced at home, and it was magnified by my experiences in school with my administrator, teachers, and peers. Trauma is real, and the side effects may not manifest immediately. As a student, I didn't know what to do with my feelings or how to explain to my teachers what was happening in my personal life at home. I wished someone would have dug deeper so I could have had a positive outlet and a sense of support.

My experience in middle school shaped who I became as an educator. I made a vow that I would look past disruptive student behaviors to determine what they *really* wanted or needed me to know. In some cases, there was nothing to their behavior other than them wanting attention—because, as you know, some attention is better than no attention. But there were also those students who really wanted someone to listen to them. Someone to notice they were hurting. Someone to take a genuine interest in them and what was happening in their world. They wanted someone to know that their anger, their hurt, and their lashing out were not personal, but they knew no other way to express themselves (Battle, 2020). Those students needed someone to extend them grace so they could work through the issues that had nothing to do with school—so they could get to the business of school.

My first group of students showed me the value of authentic, trusting relationships. Once I took the time to get to know my students, the rest of my school year took a turn for the better, and I truly enjoyed watching my students grow into learners. Over the years, I grew to love my students' willingness to trust me enough to take risks with their learning. It was rewarding to see students who were initially unsure of themselves flourish into learners who enjoyed working through tasks that challenged their thinking. This is the experience I wish for you, and in this book, I aim to show you the power of being a teacher your students know they can trust. We'll begin by learning a little about the power of relationships and trust, and how the contents of this book can help you make a positive impact on your students.

The Power of Relationships

I understand you may be somewhat weary of hearing about the influence of the teacher-student relationship and its effect on your students' social, emotional, and academic success. However, what if that is the missing piece of your students' journey? As teachers, we too often make assumptions about our students' behaviors without thinking there could be root causes of which we're unaware, that our students don't know how to communicate to us. Many students don't have a trusting adult relationship outside of school. They're dealing with serious challenges in their lives, and school can feel like just one more responsibility. For learning to occur, school must be a place where your students feel safe, seen, and heard so they can focus on their academics. If they are dealing with some of the same challenges in school that they deal with outside of school, homework is the last thing they want to think about.

Establishing strong and trusting relationships can help students feel safe to be themselves in your classroom. In his book, *Embracing Relational Teaching*, Anthony Reibel (2023) discusses the value of relational teachers:

> **Relational teachers create this kind of learning space for students, not only to make meaning, but to also develop foundational relationships that can serve as a steady reminder to students that when they face challenges or setbacks, their teacher is there to support them. (p. 21)**

Your students need the assurance that you are there for them and are rooting for their success.

The Impact of a Great Teacher

When you think about your favorite teacher when you were in school, what first comes to mind? Is it that they knew how to teach their content, or is it more about how they made you feel in their classroom? You may remember that your favorite teacher really loved teaching their subject and had high expectations for all students. But beyond that, do you also remember how you felt safe, seen, and heard in their classroom? The impact of a great teacher goes beyond their content knowledge; a great teacher strives to create a sense of belonging and emotional connection with every student they teach. As educators, it's important to consider the importance of this connection because we often underestimate the lasting impact we have on students through our everyday interactions. Our actions shape our students' memories and perceptions about themselves and about learning, whether positive or negative.

Every word, action, and gesture has the power to leave a mark. Words can encourage our students to take risks while embracing the challenges of learning, or they can discourage our students altogether. You have the power to instill a sense of confidence in your students each day they step into your classroom. To do this, you must create an environment that is inclusive and promotes a sense of belonging among all students, so they feel safe, seen, and heard. This type of environment encourages students to take risks by asking questions and sharing their thoughts and perspectives in classroom discussions and activities. In a classroom where students don't feel as if they belong, they are not likely to share their thoughts about the academic content because of the potential opinions of their peers. And how will that effect their learning?

Your impact on your students also extends beyond the classroom. It will affect their confidence, influence how they see learning, and have the potential to influence their future endeavors. As an educator, you have the privilege and responsibility to help mold students' minds as well as their hearts. You will leave a lasting impression on your students and impact the type of person they may become. This is a responsibility you shouldn't take lightly; rather, you should see it as one of the most important jobs there is. Make sure the impact you leave is meaningful and encourages your students to strive to reach their full potential.

The IMPACT Framework

This book follows my IMPACT Framework, which consists of six elements that teachers can use as guidance to improve their relationships with students and ultimately have a positive impact on students' learning experiences. I created this framework to help address the disconnect so many students feel in the classroom, as I did, because of a lack of communication, connection, and understanding. I also want educators to understand the power they have in their everyday interactions with students and be able to harness their influence to help students feel a sense of belonging in the classroom. It is through these everyday interactions that our students develop a sense of who we are as people, not only as teachers. At the heart of every relationship are people who consider each other's needs, to ensure everyone feels valued. The teacher-student relationship is no different.

The Trusted Teacher, written for secondary educators, can help you learn how to make an impact in everyday interactions with your students. These interactions don't require any additional money, but they do require teachers to look beyond conventional student narratives and recognize that connection before correction will help alleviate some of their most challenging behaviors (Jung, 2023).

While the information in this book could benefit all teachers with some modifications based on the grade level, this book is best suited for secondary teachers who seek to address the social and emotional wellness needs of their students without additional curriculum. This book will help you identify those practices you already use in your classroom but that lack consistency or intention. The goal of this book is to help you intentionally look for opportunities to address the needs of your students through deliberate selection of readings, reflections, activities, and resources.

About This Book

Each chapter of this book explores one of the six elements of the IMPACT Framework and details the practices that build a stronger teacher-student relationship and foster a positive learning environment. The framework elements and chapter descriptions are as follows.

INTENTIONAL: Great things don't happen by chance—they are planned. You can't leave it up to chance that you will address the social-emotional needs of your students. Chapter one will help you intentionally plan for addressing students' needs.

MEANINGFUL: You must ensure your practices are created and enacted with students in mind. Your content must correlate with the state standards, yes, but it also must be relevant to your students' lives, communities, or career aspirations. Chapter two will help you ensure your content is meaningful.

PRACTICAL: The best strategies are practical and can be implemented in the classroom with few to no modifications. Chapter three focuses on easy-to-use classroom practices that can improve your relationships with students and foster a positive learning environment.

AUTHENTIC: Your students don't need you to put on a show to impress them, but they do want to know that how you show up each day is who you really are. Chapter four will help you bring your authentic self into the classroom, in a manner that encourages and inspires respect.

CONSISTENT: For any structure, strategy, or intervention to work, you must be willing to consistently implement it and follow through. Your consistency lets your students know your expectations, that they can trust you, and sets the tone of the classroom. Chapter five will explore methods for ensuring your teaching practices are consistent.

TEAMWORK: Our work is inextricable from our larger school communities of teachers, staff, and families. Chapter six focuses on the benefits of working as a collective and pooling your strategies, resources, and tools to address students' needs.

Each chapter begins with a personal story from my time in the classroom that relates to the chapter topic and illustrates the important role teachers play in addressing students' needs. I know that you have had similar experiences and face similar challenges, as we work to holistically teach our students while embedding social-emotional wellness skills into our content. Each chapter then dives into the content and provides opportunities to reflect on the research, tools, and strategies presented. You or your team can modify each resource as needed to meet your school community's needs.

At the end of each chapter, you'll find a reproducible list of ten reflective questions, called "Check Your Impact." You can take the time to write out answers for these questions in a journal or elsewhere, or you can simply use the questions as food for thought as you work through that portion of the IMPACT Framework. The "Check Your Impact" questions can also be a great tool for a book study.

My hope is that you find this book beneficial and use it as a go-to resource when you need strategies, tools, and resources to address the social-emotional and academic needs of your students and build more trusting relationships with them. Relationships are created through everyday moments, so take each moment as an opportunity to ensure your students know you are there for them, as their trusted teacher.

INTENTIONAL

MEANINGFUL

PRACTICAL

AUTHENTIC

CONSISTENT

TEAMWORK

Make Intentional Choices

One day, when I was a teacher, I was driving home after a long day with my son, Maxwell. I had always dreamed of having at least one of my children at the same school as me, so I was excited to have Maxwell as a student in my fifth-grade reading class. What I hadn't anticipated was that our relationship would offer a different level of trust, honesty, and feedback. Because I was his mom first, he felt comfortable giving me feedback on my teaching—whether the feedback was positive or not—and on that day, our conversation went like this.

"Momma, today's lesson didn't really make sense." This is something we, as educators, think we are ready to hear, until we hear it. But since we were driving home, there was no escaping the conversation, so I asked him what he meant. Maxwell proceeded to tell me that the lesson just didn't make sense, and he left class confused, not knowing how to complete his homework. Maxwell was one of my highest-performing students, so I knew that if I confused him, the other students would also be confused.

INTENTIONAL

MEANINGFUL

PRACTICAL

AUTHENTIC

CONSISTENT

TEAMWORK

INTENTIONAL

MEANINGFUL

PRACTICAL

AUTHENTIC

CONSISTENT

TEAMWORK

I had a choice to make that evening. I could either go back to school the next day and proceed with the lesson as planned, considering I had already prepared the materials for the week. Or, I could revisit the lesson and make the necessary adjustments to meet my students' needs. My philosophy as an educator has always been to approach each lesson as if your own child was sitting in your class. And now, he was. That evening, I made the decision to revisit the lesson and make the necessary changes to ensure I was explicitly teaching my students what they needed so they could understand the content and complete their assignments successfully.

When I got to class the next day, I did a quick poll to see how many of my students were just as confused as Maxwell. Sure enough, many students were confused, and only a few of them understood the lesson. From that day forward, I was intentional about making sure my students were at the forefront of any lesson I planned. That included making sure my classroom felt like a safe place, where my students could be as open and honest about their understanding as my son was.

Even though I felt I had created an environment where my students could share their misconceptions and confusion during instruction, my students must not have felt the same. I often wonder how my students would have performed instructionally for the remainder of the year if I hadn't had that conversation with them after my talk with Maxwell. It is important that we seek to create a high-expectations environment, but we must provide our students the tools and resources they need to meet those expectations. This helps them understand that you have their best interests in mind. That trust creates a layer of safety inside of the classroom. "Creating a sense of emotional safety for students is central to learning, and one of the most critical challenges for teachers and instructional leaders today" (Stafford-Brizard, 2024). As you continue reading this chapter, ask yourself, "In what ways do I intentionally ensure my classroom is a safe space for my students?"

This chapter will explore the first aspect of the IMPACT Framework, *intentionality*, why it's important, and how using intentional practices can help you build stronger relationships with students.

Intentional Practices Create a Safe Classroom

Oxford Languages defines *intentional* as, "done on purpose; deliberate" (Oxford Languages, n.d.). It's an action one knowingly chooses to take. That includes the actions you take inside of your classroom. As classroom teachers, it is important that we take intentional steps to create an environment where students feel safe, supported, and seen. One of the ways we do this is by ensuring our content meets our students' needs, as in my and Maxwell's classroom. But another significant way we help students feel safe and seen is to ensure we address the social and emotional needs of our students.

Writing for Fordham Institute, Adam Tyner (2021) notes that a critical aspect of student development is feeling safe and valued. This research also shows that students' learning suffers when they don't feel safe or feel their teachers hold them to low expectations. Students are more likely to be active participants in class discussions, ask clarifying questions, and express themselves to their teachers and peers when there is a sense of belonging inside of the classroom (Tyner, 2021).

The Center for Academic, Social, and Emotional Learning (CASEL) defines *social and emotional learning* (SEL) as the process through which people acquire and apply the knowledge, skills, and attitudes to develop healthy identities, manage emotions and achieve personal and collective goals, feel and show empathy for others, establish and maintain supportive relationships, and make responsible and caring decisions (CASEL, n.d.b). SEL is an important aspect of education and human development, and it allows students to acquire and apply the skills needed to manage behavior and emotions while developing a healthy identity and outlook (CASEL, n.d.b).

The five core areas of SEL competence are self-awareness, self-management, responsible decision making, social awareness, and relationship skills. By embedding SEL in our classroom instruction, we create an inclusive learning environment that promotes the development of the SEL competencies (CASEL, n.d.b). These skills directly contribute to a person's overall success in school and life.

INTENTIONAL

MEANINGFUL

PRACTICAL

AUTHENTIC

CONSISTENT

TEAMWORK

Just as we take an intentional approach to addressing the academic needs of our students, we must also be intentional when addressing their social-emotional needs. This is especially important for those students who come to our classrooms lacking basic SEL skills and are more than likely to not have those skills addressed elsewhere. We may unconsciously label students who lack SEL skills as having behavior problems, not realizing that those students may see their behavior, even if it is inappropriate, as normal. Students who lack SEL skills have trouble following directions, participating in learning tasks, and are more likely to face rejection from their peers in comparison to classmates who have had healthy SEL skills development (Ho & Funk, 2018).

Trauma is another major factor to consider that can impact students' classroom behaviors. In their book, *The School Wellness Wheel*, Mike Ruyle, Libby Child, and Nancy Dome (2022) identify trauma as traumatic events that occur in childhood and adolescence, such as experiencing physical, emotional, or sexual abuse; witnessing violence in the home; having a family member attempt or die by suicide; and growing up in a household with substance use, mental health problems, or instability due to parental death, separation, divorce, or incarceration. Scott Ervin (2022) notes that students who have experienced trauma need to have specific procedures and strategies in the classroom to feel safe and calm. Often, when these students act on their emotions, their behavior is seen as something that needs to be punished, versus seeing the behavior as an indication that they would benefit from engaging in SEL instruction alongside their content.

When we teach our students social-emotional skills, we equip them with the tools and strategies they need to not only navigate school, but also to navigate life. If we intentionally plan and embed those social-emotional skills in our day, we can level the playing field for those students who may not get that type of support elsewhere. The Early Intervention Foundation (Clarke et al., 2021) finds that students who are in situations that make them more likely to develop emotional and behavioral issues benefit from universal mental health interventions. Universal mental health interventions, contrary to targeted interventions, are those delivered to all students. By using interventions that address all students, those students in particularly challenging situations are less likely to feel singled out or face the stigma of being in a program that not all students participate in (Hayes et al., 2023).

Intentional Practices Support SEL

Teachers can support equity and help students overcome barriers to academic success by recognizing and addressing the unique challenges students face and equipping them with the skills needed to navigate school. Figure 1.1 shows some of the most common supports schools tend to implement when addressing the SEL needs of their students.

Support Type	Intended Outcomes	Unintended Outcomes
PBIS	Improve emotional competence, academic success, and school climate	Manipulation of student behavior Stress and anxiety when students do not meet expectations
Behavior Interventionists	Monitor and address student behaviors	Students may perceive as punitive
SEL Program Curriculum	Help students develop SEL competencies through direct instruction	Teachers may perceive as an additional responsibility and may not teach it with full fidelity
Advisor Period	Connect students with assigned staff to address student concerns while addressing SEL competencies	Tends to be used as a free period if there is no administration oversight or designated program in place
Guidance Counseling Support Groups	Cultivate relationships and develop student SEL competencies using a group mode	Sessions may be interrupted based on counselor responsibilities and schoolemergencies

Figure 1.1: Common SEL supports and outcomes.

Positive Behavioral Interventions and Supports (PBIS) is a tiered framework for supporting students' behavioral, academic, social, emotional, and mental health (Center on Positive Behavioral Interventions and Supports, 2023).

When implemented schoolwide and districtwide with fidelity, PBIS improves social-emotional competence, academic success, and school climate (Center on Positive Behavioral Interventions and Supports, 2023).

Most schools use PBIS to curb unwanted behaviors in lieu of addressing the behaviors and equipping students with an alternative way to express and regulate their own behavior. Even though PBIS has a reward system embedded in the program, in my experience most teachers use it to manipulate student behavior in their favor. This type of programming does not necessarily create a safe, supportive environment where students feel valued and respected. In some cases, this type of programming can cause unwanted stress, anxiety, and behaviors when students are unable to perform up to the teachers' expectations and are penalized for displaying unwanted behaviors.

In some instances, schools opt to hire a behavior interventionist, a person hired to specifically deal with disruptive behaviors within the school. They work closely with school administrators to create and implement policies that are meant to curb those behaviors in the school that interrupt the learning environment. Behavior interventionists may also be referred to as behavior specialists in some school districts, but their function is the same. Behavior interventionists may also work alongside teachers providing training, support, and strategies to help manage unwanted student behavior in the classroom (West Virginia Department of Education, n.d.).

An issue some behavior interventionists may encounter is students may see them as an extension of administration, only available to give punitive consequences, instead of as another layer of support. Schools may also place behavior interventionists in their buildings to help monitor and address student behaviors but fail to recognize that students may see those initiatives as punitive rather than supportive if the only task they have is to administer consequences (West Virginia Department of Education, n.d.). To combat that perspective, it would benefit the school community if the behavior interventionist intentionally fostered community through initiatives that are meant to promote collaboration among teachers and students. It is important for behavior interventionists to recognize this and make an intentional effort to establish relationships with students even while dealing with negative behaviors.

With an increased need to support all students, schools may also implement SEL program curriculum that is used at specific times of the day. SEL curriculums use a specific methodology to address the SEL needs of students. These curriculums provide teachers a structured way to teach students how to identify and process the CASEL SEL competencies.

Advisor period is another way schools try to support students' SEL needs. During this period students are placed in groups and with an advisor who may or may not be their teacher throughout the day. Students meet with the advisor daily at a set time to either discuss the problems they face as students, complete lessons in their SEL curriculum, or they may just spend this time building a relationship with an adult in the school. This relationship is meant to provide students with at least one person they feel they can talk with or turn to if they are having a problem they may not know how to solve.

Guidance counseling support groups have been used to address the SEL needs of students in a whole group setting. During these support groups, guidance counselors choose a topic they will focus on for the entire group. The topics may not be specific to issues students may be having but more general in nature based on the age and grade level of the students. The purpose of the groups is to address the needs of students more universally while allowing students to see the guidance counselor as someone they can trust if they have a problem arise.

What are the most common supports implemented in your school?

_____

_____

_____

_____

_____

_____

_____

_____

_____

INTENTIONAL

MEANINGFUL

PRACTICAL

AUTHENTIC

CONSISTENT

TEAMWORK

Do you find them effective? Why or why not?

_____

_____

_____

_____

_____

_____

_____

_____

_____

What other supports do you think would address the social-emotional wellness needs of your students?

_____

_____

_____

_____

_____

_____

_____

_____

_____

Strategies to Address Students' SEL Needs

The following are some strategies that can help you meet students' SEL needs and foster a safe classroom environment.

▶ **Establish clear expectations for student behavior:** When establishing expectations, it is important to consistently adhere to consequences for inappropriate behavior and acknowledge desired student behavior. As teachers, it is vital we model the behavior we would like our students to display—behaviors such as respect, courtesy, active listening, and the ability to self-correct when we have made mistakes.

- **Take time to foster relationships with students:** Mutual, trusting relationships with students are not created overnight, so don't get discouraged if it takes time to establish authentic relationships. Consider actions such as the following.

  → Show a genuine interest in student hobbies and life outside of school.

  → Take opportunities to attend after-school events your students will be participating in.

  → If the chance arises, sponsor a school club that is not necessarily content related. This is especially effective if you are passionate about your club. One year, I sponsored the cooking club at my middle school and taught the students to cook some of my favorite dishes. It was one of the most popular clubs in the school.

- **Look for opportunities to incorporate SEL skills every day in your classroom:** This may mean taking five minutes to discuss the SEL competencies—self-awareness, self-management, responsible decision making, social awareness, and relationship skills—when the opportunity arises. One thing to remember is that these opportunities usually are preceded by an authentic teacher-student relationship. The following are a couple of ideas.

  → When teaching new content, discuss how you felt when you learned it and the strategies you used to manage the anxiety or frustration of trying to learn something new.

  → When tensions rise in the classroom, take time to discuss the importance of controlling our emotions in a variety of situations so they are not blown out of proportion. This also lends itself to discussing responsible decision making and how it only takes one bad decision to change the course of one's life.

- **Plan instruction that requires students to work alongside peers:** Not only must students develop a relationship with their teacher, but they also must foster healthy relationships among peers. Look for ways to group students in a variety of pairings to allow them the opportunity to work with classmates they may not choose to work with on their own. Build in time to incorporate team-building activities that may or may not be content driven. It is hard to bully someone you have a common interest with.

▸ **Support students when they need it:** Some students may need a trusted adult to help them work through everyday situations. Keep an eye out for ways to be that support. Some students may have needs that you are unable to address personally, but you may be able to provide them with resources to get those needs addressed. You may connect students with the guidance counselor, school social worker, or another trusted adult in your school building.

We recognize and understand that our students face social and emotional challenges, but we may not always feel at liberty or even know how to address those issues, so we tend to ignore them until they disrupt our daily classroom environment. As student behavior becomes more explosive, it can feel as if developing a healthy teacher-student relationship is impossible. Many districts suggest taking the first couple of weeks to build relationships with your students but don't give many options beyond that time. So, educators are left trying to figure out how to continue building relationships with students who may or may not have been in their classroom the first couple weeks of school.

Think about a close relationship you have with someone. I can guarantee it took more than two weeks and team-building activities to develop. Our relationships with our students are the same way. We are meeting most of our students for the first time. Some of our students come from less-than-desirable environments where they can't trust anyone around them—so why do we expect them to open up and trust us in a matter of two weeks?

Use the checklist in Figure 1.2 to reflect on how often you intentionally plan moments to address students' social-emotional learning skills.

Intention	Always	Usually	Sometimes	Never
I consider students' individual needs and differences.				
I integrate SEL skills into instruction and activities.				
I provide opportunities for students to express their emotions in a safe space.				
I incorporate discussions in my instruction that embed SEL skills.				
I address issues and conflicts in the classroom with an SEL focus.				
I am aware of my students' SEL skills growth and foster the skills by embedding them into my instruction.				
I provide opportunities for peer-to-peer collaboration.				
My students have a safe space to go when instruction is overwhelming.				
I use unplanned opportunities when they arise to incorporate SEL skills into my instruction.				
I include opportunities for students to find relevance to the content and share their connections, such as hobbies, family, community, or career aspirations.				

Figure 1.2: Intentional SEL planning checklist.

*Visit **go.SolutionTree.com/SEL** for a free reproducible version of this figure.*

INTENTIONAL

MEANINGFUL

PRACTICAL

AUTHENTIC

CONSISTENT

TEAMWORK

INTENTIONAL

MEANINGFUL

PRACTICAL

AUTHENTIC

CONSISTENT

TEAMWORK

Based on your responses in Figure 1.2 (page 19), have you intentionally defined specific SEL goals and outcomes for your students?

_____

_____

_____

_____

_____

_____

_____

_____

_____

_____

How well do you assess the social-emotional needs of your students and tailor your instruction to meet those needs? How could you improve?

_____

_____

_____

_____

_____

_____

_____

_____

_____

_____

Closing Thoughts

Educational researcher John Hattie (2023) ranks the influences he identified as having a positive or negative effect on student academic outcomes, with influences measuring 0.40 and above being deemed as contributing to at least one year of academic growth for students. Two of the influences he studies are the teacher-student relationship and teacher subject matter knowledge. The teacher-student relationship measured at 0.62 (Hattie, 2023), which demonstrates that this relationship plays a significant role in student success. On the other hand, teacher subject matter knowledge measured at 0.13 (Hattie, 2023). This statistic may surprise many educators who feel their knowledge supersedes the relationship they have with their students.

As I became more experienced teaching reading, that became my focus, *teaching reading*, and ensuring my students were growing in that area. I was still just as intentional about setting up the classroom procedures and routines needed to achieve the culture necessary to foster learner independence and order in my classroom. I will dive deeper into the importance of consistency in implementing procedures and routines in chapter 5 (page 103). However, I had to reflect on how intentional I had been to create an environment where my students felt safe, valued, and comfortable in expressing how they felt. As the teacher in the classroom, I recognized it was my responsibility to cultivate an environment where my students' SEL skills were being addressed, just as I addressed their academic needs, because the student-teacher relationship plays a significant role in the academic success of our students.

We don't all have the luxury of having our children in class to clue us into those times when we felt like we had a top-notch lesson, only to find out on test day that the lesson didn't make any sense and went over everyone's head. We look at the standards, curriculum, and pacing guide thinking we know exactly how to approach each lesson, but we often don't consider the social-emotional aspect of planning instruction. When we address our students' SEL needs and work to build SEL skills, we communicate to them that we not only value their academic progress—we also value them as individuals whose social and emotional well-being is just as important as the content we teach.

INTENTIONAL

MEANINGFUL

PRACTICAL

AUTHENTIC

CONSISTENT

TEAMWORK

Chapter 1: Check Your IMPACT

1. How can I gain an awareness of my students' life experiences? Do I know if my students have faced high levels of trauma?

   _____

   _____

   _____

   _____

   _____

   _____

   _____

2. In what ways do I make my class expectations clear, or is there still a level of ambiguity?

   _____

   _____

   _____

   _____

   _____

   _____

   _____

3. In what ways can I look for opportunities to get to know my students beyond my classroom?

   _____

   _____

   _____

   _____

   _____

   _____

   _____

4. In what ways do I take opportunities to insert SEL references into my classroom instruction without it feeling forced?

   _____

   _____

   _____

   _____

   _____

   _____

   _____

5. How do I know if my students feel safe asking me for support?

_____

_____

_____

_____

_____

_____

_____

6. How often do I intentionally plan tasks that require students to work with peers to foster student-student relationships?

_____

_____

_____

_____

_____

_____

_____

7. How often do I provide students with the needed support to be successful in my classroom?

_____

_____

_____

_____

_____

_____

_____

8. How do I address unwanted behaviors when they occur and assign consequences as appropriate?

_____

_____

_____

_____

_____

_____

_____

9. When do I use school-based supports to address my students' social, emotional, and academic needs?

_____

_____

_____

_____

_____

_____

_____

10. What opportunities do I take to monitor my students' progress to recognize when adjustments to instructional plans need to be made?

_____

_____

_____

_____

_____

_____

_____

INTENTIONAL

MEANINGFUL

PRACTICAL

AUTHENTIC

CONSISTENT

TEAMWORK

Plan Meaningful Instruction

"You still think you're the ultimate OG?" This was a direct message I received over social media on a random day in August. Once I got over the slight shock of the message, I realized it was sent from a student I had taught ten years before, Jaime. The message was actually a playful nod to the relationship I had with my students that year. Although I was surprised to hear from him, I have fond memories of him and his classmates. This class of students was one that helped me realize the power of authentic relationship building.

The year I taught Jaime, a large population of Latino students had just graduated from the English as a second language (ESL) program and were placed in my English language arts (ELA) classroom. Because I had not previously had many Latino students in my classroom, I made it a priority to get to know my new students and learn about their cultures so I could best address their needs. I decided to use Hispanic Heritage Month as a way for my students and I to learn about Latino students' heritage using literature and ELA tasks.

INTENTIONAL

MEANINGFUL

PRACTICAL

AUTHENTIC

CONSISTENT

TEAMWORK

I was able to achieve my skills and objectives, with slight tweaks to the content, and make it a broader learning opportunity.

Though I used this month as an opportunity to begin learning about their culture, I continued to embed culturally rich material into my content throughout the year. This not only allowed me to address my own misunderstandings about my students' respective cultures, but it also allowed me to build relationships with them and their families, culminating in an end-of-unit celebration. During this celebration, I invited my students and their families to bring in their favorite dish. They couldn't wait to share! This didn't just benefit my Latino students; it benefited all my students. Whenever you can find a teaching moment to embed your students' cultures, traditions, or interests into your content, seize the opportunity. It not only gives students a sense of validation and inclusion, it also gives them an opportunity to expand on the content from a personal perspective.

It helps to allow students to get to know you as a person beyond the teacher in the classroom—because relationships are not one-sided. In my classroom, each morning as I transitioned from one task to another, I mentioned something I did or saw the evening before to engage my students in a brief conversation before we began our next task. This type of sharing opens the door for students to share their experiences. If my students played sports on the weekend, I made sure to ask about their games or their weekend visits with relatives. We may think that building relationships with our students takes more than us simply being ourselves and allowing our students to get to know us, but it often doesn't. Simple moments of connection like this, and being consistent in how you treat students, significantly contribute to developing authentic, trusting relationships.

As the school year progresses, your students' true personalities begin to show. In Jaime's case, he appeared to be somewhat shy, but he would crack a joke to break awkward moments in the classroom. He was not disruptive, nor did he share much about his family, but he knew when to insert a punchline to make the class laugh. One spring day, Jaime's mother brought me a dozen roses to school because he had told her how often I talked about the flowers in my home garden. He told her I seemed so happy whenever I talked about my garden and thought I would enjoy the roses because they were beautiful. The simple moments of me sharing my hobbies, exciting news, and, most of all, my accomplishments made the biggest impression on my students. Students recognize that we all have moments of joy, sadness, and opportunities to celebrate, and my students felt safe enough to share those moments with me and their classmates.

When Jaime reached out, ten years later, he shared with me how he had never forgotten how supported he had felt in my class. His message was a special reminder that we as educators don't just connect with students for 180 days; we can connect with them for a lifetime. Our everyday interactions help shape their outlook on school and relationships with their teachers and classmates. Educators must strive to connect with our students and ensure what we do in the classroom has relevance for them.

This chapter will explore the second aspect of the IMPACT Framework, *meaningful* practices, and how our students' needs and interests must be at the forefront of our decisions. It is one thing to simply plan an activity, but the activity takes on an entirely different meaning when students see how they are represented in the planning. As you look to build trusting relationships with your students, allowing them to feel seen and valued in their content has a major impact on how they feel in the overall classroom environment. Take a moment to reflect on how you create the lesson plans for your curriculum. Do you take opportunities to insert your students' cultures, traditions, or hobbies in the plan, or do you stick to the script? As you read through this chapter, think about ways you can ensure your students are represented in your instruction and everyday interactions.

Relationships Matter for Meaningful Instruction

"Students don't care what you know until they know that you care," as the saying goes. These words capture the foundation of our journey as educators. It is vital for us to invest time in building authentic, trusting relationships with our students beyond the first two weeks of school. By doing so, we gain valuable information that enables us to align our teaching practices with our students' cultures, traditions, and interests. While we understand the need to teach content at face value, we must seize every opportunity to make it relevant and meaningful for our students when the opportunity presents itself.

We must consider our students as we plan our instruction. It is difficult to recognize and understand how to plan instruction for students we really don't know. As educators, it is important we recognize that fostering relationships with our students both allows us the opportunity to address their SEL needs and gives us the insights we need to meet the academic needs of our students. We can't discount the power of feeling seen and included, and the teacher-student relationship is at the heart of this feeling. We should embrace opportunities to transform the lives of our students by creating meaningful, real-world, and impactful learning experiences.

To achieve meaningful connections between content and students' lives, educators should adopt a student-centered approach that acknowledges students' diverse backgrounds, interests, and perspectives. By actively seeking out real-world opportunities, teachers can contextualize their lessons and foster a sense of relevance and authenticity in the classroom. In her article, "Teach Up for Equity and Excellence," educator Carol Ann Tomlinson (2023) cites Helen Hodges's 2001 work, which determines that when a strong connection between home and the classroom exists, student cognition (thinking) and metacognition (thinking about thinking) improve because students feel the tasks are authentic and purposeful. As we continue to look for ways to encourage students to take ownership of their learning, we must recognize that our students want to engage in learning that has a direct connection to their life experiences, future career goals, or real-world situations.

Prioritizing Students' Needs and Interests

In his book, *Closing the Attitude Gap*, Principal Baruti K. Kafele (2013) asserts the importance of what students see, hear, feel, and experience in the classroom because it is the students' overall experience that determines how well they connect with the teacher and the content. Our content knowledge is not the only thing that matters when we are teaching students. What also matters is that students recognize they're at the forefront of your planning. Tomlinson (2023) explains that teachers who "teach up" with a focus on student equity and high ceilings of learning consistently create environments where students can create a bond of trust with their teachers and peers using the content and learning environment as the catalyst because students recognize the connection between their lives, experiences, and the content. This, in turn, inspires and motivates students to persist through the task of learning. It may seem a bit overwhelming to think that instruction goes beyond the content, but as educators, we prepare our students for life beyond the classroom. We are helping foster an appreciation of learning from a variety of perspectives that will be valuable to them throughout the rest of their lives.

The following are five questions you can ask yourself during the planning process to intentionally plan meaningful instruction around your students' needs and interests.

1. **How do I incorporate the diverse perspectives and experiences of my students in my content to make it more relevant and engaging?** As you plan your lessons, take into consideration ways to incorporate student or community perspectives into your instruction. The "Student Inventory Form," featured later in this chapter (page 43), is a helpful tool for getting started. Can you begin with a community partner showing a direct correlation between the community and your content and end with students explaining their understanding of the content and how it relates to their lives?

2. **What strategies do I incorporate that create a supportive environment where all students feel included, valued, and respected?** Take an opportunity to reflect on the strategies that you have implemented in the classroom to build community and ensure all students feel as if they belong, are being respected, and their voices are heard. If you see students who shy away from participating in class discussions or are apprehensive about sharing, research additional ways to create a classroom environment where all students feel valued.

3. **How often do I regularly assess my students' progress and adjust my instruction accordingly to ensure all students can perform at their highest potential?** An important part of the learning process is regular checks for understanding to determine whether learning is progressing as planned. Review your lesson plans to identify opportunities to insert these checks to judge student progress toward mastery. This will assist you in determining whether adjustments to

INTENTIONAL
MEANINGFUL
PRACTICAL
AUTHENTIC
CONSISTENT
TEAMWORK

instruction are necessary before you assess students at the end of your instruction and learn they missed key skills and concepts.

4. **What technology can I incorporate into my instruction to enhance accessibility and engagement?** How will you use technology as a means for students to demonstrate mastery of content? As we continue to evolve as a technological society, we need to provide students with authentic ways to incorporate technology into their daily classroom instruction beyond taking assessments and submitting assignments. Can students create a thirty-second commercial instead of writing an essay? What about allowing students to interview members of the school community to discuss pressing issues and broadcast it for the student body to watch? Is there an opportunity for students to create a survey and post QR codes throughout the school for people to take the survey? There are many ways students can use technology in a classroom setting to see its value beyond entertainment purposes.

5. **Do I provide opportunities for students to collaborate with their peers to hear each other's unique perspectives and cultural backgrounds?** Can you structure the classroom instruction to include discussions you facilitate as the teacher but require the students to contribute their thoughts and respond to the thinking of others? You may provide the initial questions, but how can that moment be designed so the students can take it over and maintain momentum?

It is easy to fall into the routine of using the same lesson plans year after year without taking into account that our students are not the same year after year, or even class period after class period. A one-size-fits-all model does not work in the classroom.

Motivation, participation, and engagement are inextricably linked with academic achievement (Frey, Fisher, & Smith, 2019). In their book, *All Learning is Social and Emotional*, Frey and colleagues (2019) discuss the difference between performance goals and mastery goals. In essence, performance goals encourage friendly competition whereas mastery goals focus on learning for the benefit of oneself. "Students with a mastery goal mindset are more resilient and persistent in their learning, have a more positive attitude toward school, attribute their success to their effort and use cognitive and metacognitive skills effectively" (Midgley, 2020, as cited in Frey et al., 2019). Ensuring students recognize themselves in the content is one way to help shift your students' thinking around learning. How much easier would it be to help students create goals around achievement if they saw value in the content because it in some way directly relates to their lives? If your goal is to create an environment where students see themselves at the forefront of planning and feel safe going through the process of learning, we should structure our classrooms so learning does not feel as if it's measured based on performance (peer comparison), but instead is mastery focused (learning for oneself).

Students come to us with varying levels of academic and social-emotional strengths, and if we don't take both of those factors into account, we can have a classroom full of disengaged students who may not have the skills to cope with the challenges of learning. In their report, *Educating the Whole Child: Improving School Climate to Support Student Success*, Linda Darling-Hammond and Channa Cook-Harvey (2018) state:

> **Rather than assuming all children will respond to the same teaching approaches equally well, effective teachers seek to personalize supports for different children. Schools should avoid prescribing learning experiences around a mythical average. When they try to force all children to fit one sequence or pacing guide, they miss the opportunity to nurture the individual potential of every child, and they can cause children (as well as teachers) to adopt counterproductive views about themselves and their own learning potential, which undermine progress. (p. 6)**

Although our students' initial social-emotional skills are fostered in the home, our schools and classrooms will either reinforce what our students have already learned or will teach them new skills and strategies that will promote academic and social success.

When instruction is designed with students as the central focus, it sets the stage for a positive and inclusive learning environment. By recognizing and valuing the diverse experiences and cultural backgrounds of students, educators create an atmosphere that encourages collaboration, positive interactions, and mutual understanding. This environment promotes empathy, which allows students to gain insights into each other's lives, cultures, and traditions. In the same report, Darling-Hammond and Cook-Harvey (2018) also state:

> **Positive relationships, including trust in the teacher, and positive emotions—such as interest and excitement—open up the mind to learning. Negative emotions—such as fear of failure, anxiety, and self-doubt—reduce the capacity of the brain to process information and to learn. (p. 6)**

By fostering an inclusive classroom environment, students develop a greater sense of belonging and acceptance, allowing them to fully engage in their learning journey because they have a feeling of safety and trust among their peers and teacher. Let's look at how a practitioner approaches this belonging and trust in her classroom.

Intentional Practices From a Teacher's Perspective

This excerpt is from an interview with R. Miller, a tenth-grade ELA Teacher in Nashville, Tennessee (R. Miller, personal communication, July 15, 2023). She is in her fourth year in the profession and understands she must be intentional in building relationships with her students so she can challenge their thinking.

During the first days of school, I bombard students with questionnaires and quizzes that let me get to know my students' tastes and preferences in the learning environment. We take icebreakers and get-to-know-you exercises very seriously in my classroom. Learning cannot happen in isolation. We are a community of learners growing alongside one another each and every day. I allow my students to bear witness to my mistakes. I apologize to them when I'm wrong. When I ask a deep critical thinking question and the room goes silent, I often have to remind my students that there is bravery in vulnerability; someone has to be courageous enough to initiate the discussion. One timid soul will finally squeak out an answer, and I always react as if I've never heard anything more enlightening. I embed collaboration activities like think-pair-shares and turn and talks to enhance our learning community. When students are leading the discussion, students are doing the learning.

This may sound cliché, but centering student voice is so important in creating an educational experience that really encourages exploration in the classroom. I'd like to think that I model genuine curiosity by constantly questioning my students on their likes, their dislikes, their fears, and their dreams. During the school day, I am always moving about the hallways and classroom having these small interactions with my students. "What'd you do this weekend?" "How was last night's game?" "How's your little sister doing?" "What's your grade like in Biology?" Students hardly notice that I'm taking inventory that will eventually further their learning.

I would also be remiss if I failed to stress the importance of data in instructional planning. You have to be married to the numbers. Initially, I was very wary of analyzing data because, truthfully, I didn't know what it all meant. Sure, I was able to read the charts and quantify how many students were reaching various achievement levels, but I was struggling to draw the connection back to my instruction. It all finally clicked during my third year in the classroom. When students are struggling to master a specific standard, I immediately consider their specific learning preferences needs. What, specifically, is keeping this student from grasping this concept, and how can I create additional vantage points for them to access the learning? While reading Sophocles' "Oedipus the King," several of my students were struggling to identify theme as indicated by the results of the text selection exam. They were enjoying the plot of the story but couldn't quite see the bigger picture. Then, it dawned on me! I had to offer my students a choice. I expanded the final assignment to include songwriting and social media. Without consistently considering students' interests and talents, I wouldn't have been able to make the necessary pivots to ensure every student felt confident in demonstrating their learning.

Over the course of a unit, I gauge my students' interest in the content by offering surveys as exit tickets and seeking feedback from some of my most and least engaged students. I love speaking with my former students on ways to improve lessons for the upcoming year; I even invite them to return to our class and serve as peer tutors during their favorite units. This creates a network of support that reaches far beyond their classmates.

The needs of Ms. Miller's students came first during the planning process. She understood that her students needed to master her grade level standards, and they also needed to be ready to take the practice ACT in the spring—but none of that mattered if she could not connect with them beyond her content.

What is your biggest takeaway from Ms. Miller's story?

_____

_____

_____

_____

_____

_____

_____

_____

_____

What elements from Ms. Miller's practice are present in your own classroom? What new practices would you consider adopting?

_____

_____

_____

_____

_____

_____

_____

_____

_____

Strategies to Plan Meaningful Instruction

The remainder of this chapter walks through a series of actions you can take as you begin to design your instruction with the students at the forefront of your planning. Figure 2.1 is a flowchart you can use as a visual guide as you progress through this section. Consider circling the actions you want to work on.

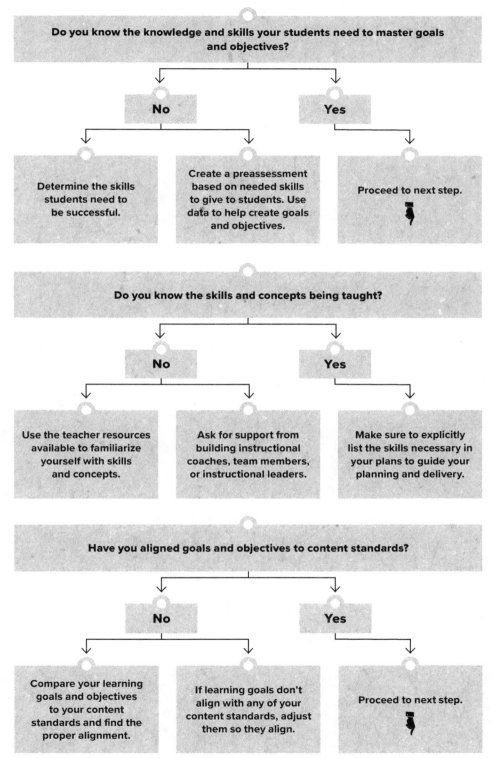

Figure 2.1: Flowchart for designing meaningful instruction.

continued →

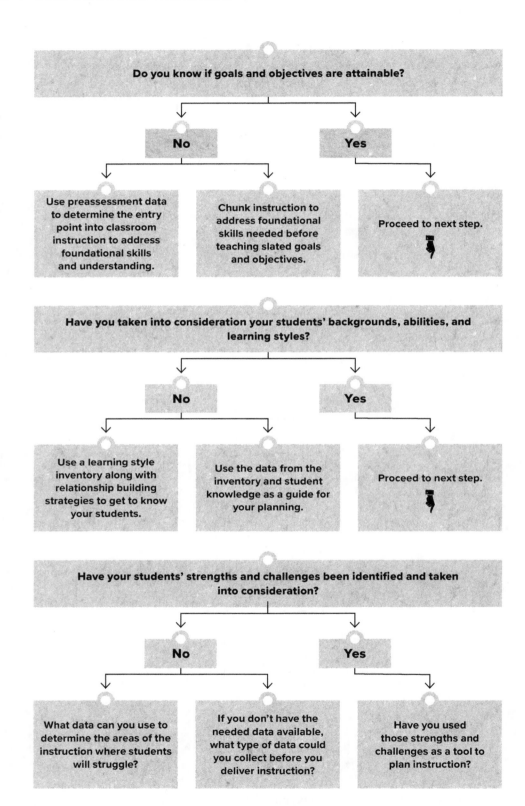

Do you know if goals and objectives are attainable?

No

Yes

Use preassessment data to determine the entry point into classroom instruction to address foundational skills and understanding.

Chunk instruction to address foundational skills needed before teaching slated goals and objectives.

Proceed to next step.

Have you taken into consideration your students' backgrounds, abilities, and learning styles?

No

Yes

Use a learning style inventory along with relationship building strategies to get to know your students.

Use the data from the inventory and student knowledge as a guide for your planning.

Proceed to next step.

Have your students' strengths and challenges been identified and taken into consideration?

No

Yes

What data can you use to determine the areas of the instruction where students will struggle?

If you don't have the needed data available, what type of data could you collect before you deliver instruction?

Have you used those strengths and challenges as a tool to plan instruction?

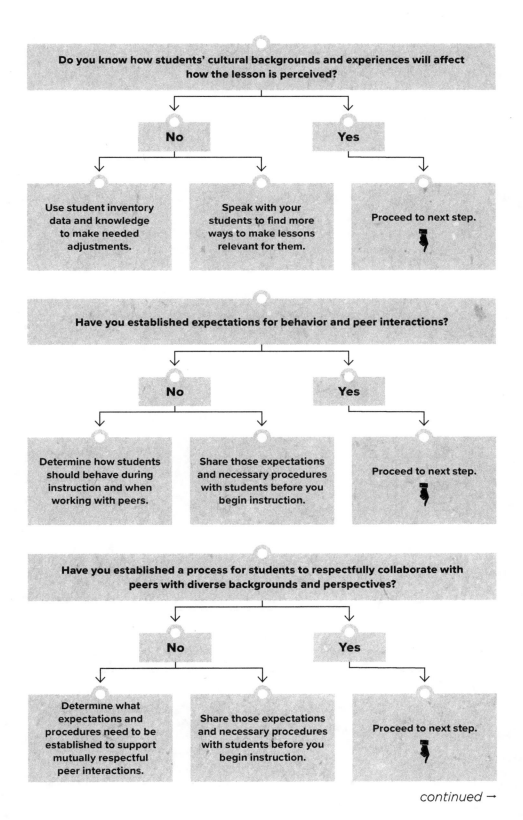

Do you know how students' cultural backgrounds and experiences will affect how the lesson is perceived?

No

Yes

Use student inventory data and knowledge to make needed adjustments.

Speak with your students to find more ways to make lessons relevant for them.

Proceed to next step.

Have you established expectations for behavior and peer interactions?

No

Yes

Determine how students should behave during instruction and when working with peers.

Share those expectations and necessary procedures with students before you begin instruction.

Proceed to next step.

Have you established a process for students to respectfully collaborate with peers with diverse backgrounds and perspectives?

No

Yes

Determine what expectations and procedures need to be established to support mutually respectful peer interactions.

Share those expectations and necessary procedures with students before you begin instruction.

Proceed to next step.

continued →

INTENTIONAL

MEANINGFUL

PRACTICAL

AUTHENTIC

CONSISTENT

TEAMWORK

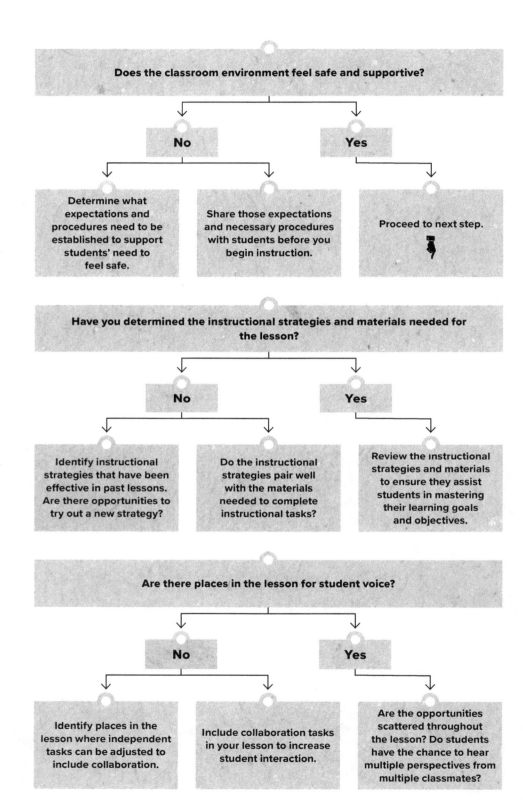

Does the classroom environment feel safe and supportive?

No

Yes

Determine what expectations and procedures need to be established to support students' need to feel safe.

Share those expectations and necessary procedures with students before you begin instruction.

Proceed to next step.

Have you determined the instructional strategies and materials needed for the lesson?

No

Yes

Identify instructional strategies that have been effective in past lessons. Are there opportunities to try out a new strategy?

Do the instructional strategies pair well with the materials needed to complete instructional tasks?

Review the instructional strategies and materials to ensure they assist students in mastering their learning goals and objectives.

Are there places in the lesson for student voice?

No

Yes

Identify places in the lesson where independent tasks can be adjusted to include collaboration.

Include collaboration tasks in your lesson to increase student interaction.

Are the opportunities scattered throughout the lesson? Do students have the chance to hear multiple perspectives from multiple classmates?

INTENTIONAL

MEANINGFUL

PRACTICAL

AUTHENTIC

CONSISTENT

TEAMWORK

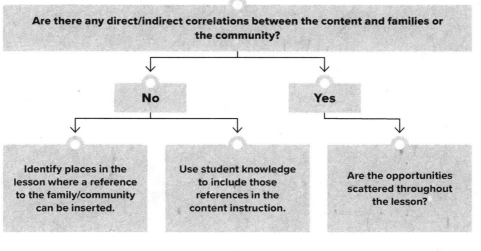

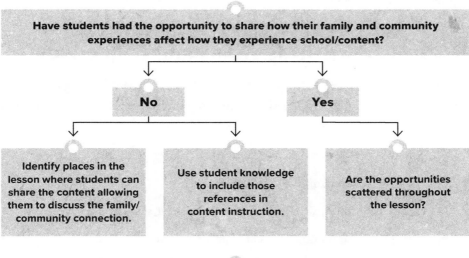

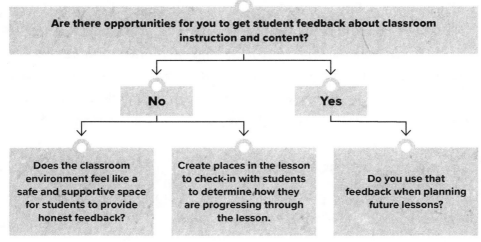

continued →

INTENTIONAL

MEANINGFUL

PRACTICAL

AUTHENTIC

CONSISTENT

TEAMWORK

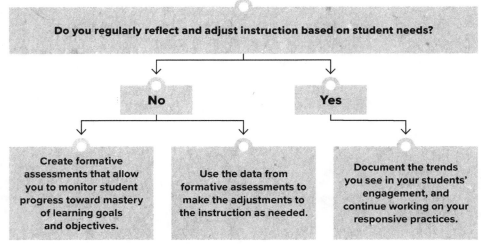

*Visit **go.SolutionTree.com/SEL** for a free reproducible version of this figure.*

Establish Learning Goals and Objectives

The first step in the planning process is to establish learning goals and objectives that are meaningful, aligned to standards, and responsive to your students' skills. Consider each of the following questions.

▶ What knowledge will students need to master goals and objectives?

▶ What skills and concepts will be taught?

▶ Are goals and objectives aligned with content standards?

▶ Are the goals and objectives attainable and measurable?

Deconstruct your content standards down to the skills and concepts that are embedded in the standard. Then, determine what skills your students will need to successfully master the standard versus the skills they will learn from your instruction. By completing this task, you will be able to see what ways you may need to differentiate the instruction based on students' current skills, and it will also help you decide what skills you may need to remediate before you begin teaching any new content.

Consider Student Population

The following questions can help you consider your students' unique abilities, strengths, and backgrounds.

▶ Have student backgrounds, abilities, and learning styles been identified?

▶ Have student strengths and challenges been identified and taken into consideration?

▶ Will their cultural backgrounds affect how the instruction is perceived?

Use the student inventory form in figure 2.2 to learn more about your students.

Student Name: _____ **Grade:** _____

1. What is your favorite hobby or interest?. _____

2. Do you play any sports? What are they? _____

3. What is your favorite place to visit? _____

4. Describe your perfect day. _____
   _____

5. Name two things that make you laugh. _____

6. What is your favorite subject in school? _____

7. Do you learn better working with a partner or alone? _____

8. Does note-taking help you learn class content? _____

9. If you had to teach our class, what activities would you have your classmates do?
   _____

10. Do you enjoy creating digital presentations? Why or why not? _____
    _____

11. If you were asked to give a presentation to the class, how would you design it?
    _____

12. What is your dream job? _____

13. What types of things do you like to read about? _____

14. Write a short paragraph about yourself. _____
    _____
    _____
    _____
    _____
    _____

Figure 2.2: Student inventory form.

*Visit **go.SolutionTree.com/SEL** for a free reproducible version of this figure.*

What skills do your students possess that will help them with the classroom content? What skills are missing that may pose a challenge during instruction?

_____
_____
_____
_____
_____
_____
_____
_____
_____
_____

How might students perceive the lesson? How can you address students' perceptions in the lesson introduction?

_____
_____
_____
_____
_____
_____
_____
_____
_____
_____

Create an Inclusive Learning Environment

After you have fully considered your student population's unique needs, the next step is to ensure there have been intentional efforts in creating a classroom environment that is positive, inclusive, and supportive of peer-to-peer interaction. You can achieve this type of environment by making your classroom expectations clear to your students. It will be beneficial to review how you expect them to behave in the classroom, toward their peers, and while using classroom materials and resources. Also implement the classroom procedures that teach students the step-by-step processes they will need in your classroom. This supports your behavior expectations because procedures explain how your students will operate, while your expectations address their behavior. Consider each of the following questions.

- ► Have expectations for behavior and peer interactions been established?

- ► How will you foster peer collaboration and the need to consider diverse perspectives?

- ► Does the classroom environment feel safe and supportive?

Incorporate Student Perspectives and Experiences

After you have established supportive and respectful class interactions through clear expectations and procedures, you can then ensure that the voices of all your students are heard and incorporated into your lessons. Consider each of the following questions.

- ► How are instructional strategies and materials selected and implemented in the classroom instruction?

- ► How do you incorporate student voice and contributions in the instructional process?

- ► What new instructional strategies do you want to try?

- ► How would you like the new strategies to affect student engagement?

- ► What new instructional materials would you like to implement?

- ► What is the outcome on student performance that you would like to see?

Include Caregivers or the Community

You've ensured that you've incorporated your students' perspectives into your lesson. The next step is to consider ways to connect to and engage with care-givers or the larger school community. Consider each of the following questions.

- ► Are there any direct or indirect correlations between content and students' families or the community?

INTENTIONAL

MEANINGFUL

PRACTICAL

AUTHENTIC

CONSISTENT

TEAMWORK

▶ Are there opportunities to include students' families or members of the community in your instructional plans?

▶ Have students had the opportunity to share how their experiences affect the way they see and value school?

Reflect and Adjust

Just because we've completed a lesson plan does not mean our work is finished. To improve, we must seek feedback from our students, not only on their learning progress, but on our instructional practices as well. Consider each of the following questions.

▶ Do you seek feedback from students to determine whether they are making progress in mastering goals and objectives?

▶ Do you regularly reflect on personal instructional practices, student motivation, and engagement?

Figure 2.3 is a form you can use to seek feedback from your students. Give this to students periodically to get a sense of how they feel their learning needs are being met. There is no place for students to write their names, so they can feel safe giving their honest opinions. Instead of looking for individual answers, look for trends in feedback. Those trends should give you enough information to adjust instruction as needed. If you want to solicit feedback from students based on a specific task or assignment, feel free to have them write their names on the form.

Closing Thoughts

Using the resources provided throughout this chapter will support your journey as you balance incorporating your students' interests, hobbies, and lives into your instruction. Intentionally looking for those moments to include your students in the content they learn turns completing assignments from being a task into an authentic learning experience they *want* to do. The goal is to help your students understand the value of education in their lives and become invested learners who look for opportunities to learn and gain new knowledge.

1. On a scale of 1 to 10 with 10 being the highest and 1 the lowest, did you feel today's lesson took into account your learning needs?

   (LOWEST) 1 — 2 — 3 — 4 — 5 — 6 — 7 — 8 — 9 — 10 (HIGHEST)

2. What parts of the lesson did you feel were less beneficial to your learning needs?

   _____

   _____

   _____

3. On a scale of 1 to 10 with 10 being the highest, how do feel the learning strategies and materials positively impacted the lesson?

   (LOWEST) 1 — 2 — 3 — 4 — 5 — 6 — 7 — 8 — 9 — 10 (HIGHEST)

4. What parts of the lesson were the most engaging? What parts of the lesson were not engaging? Why?

   _____

   _____

   _____

5. Do you feel that your voice and opinions were heard by the teacher and your peers?

   _____

6. What parts of the lesson do you feel you can use in the real-world?

   _____

   _____

   _____

7. What would you like to explore further?

   _____

   _____

   _____

   _____

   _____

8. Is there anything else you would like me to know?

   _____

   _____

   _____

   _____

   _____

Figure 2.3: Student feedback form.

*Visit **go.SolutionTree.com/SEL** for a free reproducible version of this figure.*

Chapter 2: Check Your IMPACT

1. How am I intentionally fostering an inclusive and positive learning environment?

   _____

   _____

   _____

   _____

   _____

   _____

   _____

2. How do I build authentic positive relationships with my students so I can have a better understanding of their needs?

   _____

   _____

   _____

   _____

   _____

   _____

   _____

3. In what ways do I account for the diverse backgrounds in my classroom?

   _____

   _____

   _____

   _____

   _____

   _____

   _____

4. How often do I integrate students' interests and experiences into my classroom instruction?

   _____

   _____

   _____

   _____

   _____

   _____

   _____

page 1 of 3

5. How am I supporting my students' individual learning journeys?

_____

_____

_____

_____

_____

_____

_____

6. Do I provide multiple ways for my students to demonstrate their learning? How so?

_____

_____

_____

_____

_____

_____

_____

7. How often do I solicit feedback from my students to improve my instructional practices?

_____

_____

_____

_____

_____

_____

_____

8. Is my instruction flexible enough to make adjustments to meet the needs of my students? How can I improve at this?

_____

_____

_____

_____

_____

_____

_____

9. How often do I create opportunities for my students to collaborate and learn from each other?

_____

_____

_____

_____

_____

_____

_____

10. How do I make connections between the curriculum and real-world experiences to make the content more relevant to my students?

_____

_____

_____

_____

_____

_____

_____

Use Practical Strategies

I remember walking into school one day to prepare my classroom for my students' arrival the week before they were to return. This was the day I would receive my roster of students so I could begin reviewing any information we had about them. It was my second year teaching sixth grade, and in addition to all the usual planning, I had to move to a new classroom. So you can imagine how busy I was!

Shortly after getting my roster of new students, I received a visit from two fifth-grade teachers who were going around to see which teachers received which students. As soon as they saw my roster, they noticed I had a student they'd had last year—let's call him *John*. They wanted to tell me all about John and how they just couldn't get him to learn and that he was very oppositional and disrespectful. After a couple of minutes of their commentary, I stopped them and let them know that students mature over the summer and that I didn't think I'd have the same experience.

On the first day of school, I knew exactly who John was as he walked down the hallway. He didn't have school supplies, his clothes were messy, and he had a careless demeanor. I politely stopped him at my door to say hello and that I was glad to see him. He gave me a halfhearted response and took his seat.

A couple of weeks go by, and John still didn't have school supplies and was beginning to get behind in class. So, one day after school, I gathered the supplies he needed for all his classes and placed them on his desk so they would be there when he arrived the next morning. I didn't want him to fall any further behind in any of his classes, so I made sure he had what he needed. The next morning, John was surprised to see all of his supplies on his desk, and he thanked me.

Over the next few weeks, John was still struggling to adjust to the structures in my classroom, so I asked him to stay after class to speak with me privately. I simply asked him, What was going on with his behavior? Why did he seem so upset and didn't want to participate in class? I couldn't understand why John was dismissive when assignments were given. He wasn't outwardly disrespectful toward me, but he could be toward his peers. If they said something he didn't like, they would know very quickly. Most notable was John's overall level of agitation. The smallest incident would set him off. I could tell he had not had a great experience in school so far and was not looking for that to change anytime soon. I allowed John a moment to process my question, and I didn't force him to immediately tell me what was going on. But, after a few minutes, John began to open up to me. It was clear he had been holding these feelings in and longing for a chance to get them out. He told me his mom had to abruptly leave their home and move, and he was angry. He was angry that they had to stay in a shelter for months, he was angry that he had very little clothing, and he was angry that his mother was struggling to survive.

I realized that day that John was not being defiant or disrespectful in class; he was simply coping with big emotions and significant life challenges he didn't know how to handle. He wanted to help his mom, but he was only in the sixth grade. He knew he was behind academically because of the things he was dealing with personally, but he didn't know the way forward. I'm not saying I didn't hold John responsible for his actions, because I did. But after that day, there were fewer behaviors that needed correction. I believe John knew I had his best interests at heart and wanted him to succeed academically, and he felt safe when he was in my classroom. After that day, that moment of connection, John became one of my hardest-working students, and I believe he associated my classroom with safety. I am thankful to this day that I decided to make my own connection with John, despite what his previous teachers had to say about him. Students like John will always enter our classrooms with a hard exterior, searching for that teacher who can look beyond their behaviors and see what's beneath the surface.

The third aspect of the IMPACT Framework is to ensure your classroom strategies are *practical*—that they make sense and are actionable in the context of your classroom. When you think about addressing your students' SEL needs, you must begin on a practical level. I wasn't sure what was going on with John specifically, but I knew his behavior had a root cause. I could have let the behaviors continue, but what would that have accomplished? It was practical at the time to try to help this student and improve the learning experience for him and the rest of the students. I had an opportunity to help not only John, but the energy of the classroom. John needed to feel seen, heard, and valued, and all it took was me taking time to allow him to share what he was dealing with. Some students you encounter may just need to know you care, while other students may need you to help them get school supplies so they can be successful in your classroom. As you read through the rest of this chapter, think about the practical ways you can build and foster trust among your students in your classroom.

Practicing the SEL Strategies We Want to See

As teachers, we are continually searching for practical solutions to address the social-emotional needs of students. We realize we must tend to students' needs beyond academics, but it's challenging to find a practical approach that is also easy to incorporate into classroom flow and doesn't take away from instructional time. It's not that educators don't understand that students learn best when their psychological and physical needs are met, but they are looking for ways to address them in a practical format that doesn't feel forced and is truly effective. I recognized early in my career that it is the simplest acts that go the furthest when trying to understand the actions and thinking of your students. Taking time to talk with your students in a way that is nonjudgmental pays huge dividends. Most students don't have a trusting adult to air their feelings or emotions to, so they don't always feel as if they are seen or heard. A listening ear can not only help foster trust with your students, but it will also give you some insight into your students' life experiences. Just like with John, our students are facing so many adverse experiences, and they don't know where or who to turn to. Even you, their teacher, may not appear trustworthy initially. It will take time to establish that trust, and it only requires small acts of kindness to show you truly care.

There must be a connection established, a relationship, before students will allow teachers the opportunity to truly understand the challenges they face. In her article, "Connection Before Correction," professor Lee Ann Jung (2023) states that teachers must understand why certain behaviors happen in order to create an effective plan of correction. Teachers shouldn't automatically assume students are displaying certain behaviors to purposely disrupt class. Rather, teachers should try to recognize when certain behaviors are communicating a message that the student does not know how to verbalize.

Writer Jessica Minahan (2023) states that when students engage in behavior that appears to be malicious and show no apparent remorse for their actions, it may be that the student does not have the perspective-taking skills or self-awareness to understand how their actions affect others (Bengtsson & Arvidsson, 2011, as cited in Minahan, 2023). The student has likely not been taught how to own their mistakes, empathize with others, or act with compassion. This type of behavior is more prevalent in secondary students (Bengtsson & Arvidsson, 2011; Nijhof, Te Brinke, Njardvik, & Liber, 2021, as cited in Minahan, 2023).

It is critical for educators to recognize when students lack self-awareness, which is one of the five competencies of CASEL's (n.d.b) SEL framework. If teachers can recognize this, appropriate action can be taken when students display inappropriate behavior. If we just assume students are purposely trying to hurt their peers with full awareness of their actions, we are likely to give a punitive consequence for the action instead of engaging the student in true restorative practices.

In his interview for *Educational Leadership* (McKibben & Smith, 2023), principal, author, and national presenter on restorative practices Dominique Smith asserts that educators must realize that an all-or-nothing approach is not always effective when handling student behavior because there are teachable moments even when disciplining students. When punitive consequences are the first and only means to correct undesired student behavior, we run the risk of tarnishing the teacher-student relationship. Smith does not disagree that students should be held accountable for their behaviors but rather suggests we take a moment to understand the student and the cause of the behavior before we dish out a punitive consequence.

If our goal as educators is to ensure our students are equipped with the SEL skills needed to be successful in and out of the classroom, the way we approach discipline and help our students recognize how their behavior affects others must be intentional. When we have an established connection with our students, helping them take accountability for their actions while understanding another's perspective regarding their behavior is part of the restorative process. Instead of simply punishing students with no plan of action upon their return to class, engaging them in a reflective conversation to help them gain an awareness of their actions and how they affected others before the consequence is given has a greater chance of keeping the relationship intact while helping students understand they will be held accountable for their actions (McKibben & Smith, 2023).

Strategies to Understand Student Behavior

When teachers create an environment that allows them to simultaneously de-escalate disruptive student behavior while getting to the root of the issue, they set the foundation necessary to create an environment and culture that is built on trust. The objective is to ensure students feel they are seen, heard, valued, and belong in the classroom community. When students have a sense of belonging in the classroom they feel "appreciated, validated, accepted, respected, included, supported, and treated fairly" (Barron & Kinney, 2021; Cobb & Krownapple, 2019, as cited in Chandler & Budge, 2023, p. 57). A sense of belonging can lead to "enhancements or increases to the following: pro-social classroom behavior, self-

INTENTIONAL MEANINGFUL PRACTICAL AUTHENTIC CONSISTENT TEAMWORK

esteem, self-confidence, positive peer relationships, and skills of self-man-agement" (Barron & Kinney, 2021, pp. 2–3, as cited in Chandler & Budge, 2023, p. 58).

Taking an opportunity to get to the root cause of student behavior does not exempt them from being held accountable for their actions, but rather gives you an understanding of your students' perspectives. Following are some simple strategies you can implement in your daily classroom practice to address the social-emotional needs of your students and help your students develop a sense of belonging in your classroom.

- ▸ Actively listen

- ▸ Practice empathy and validate feelings

- ▸ Model vulnerability

These strategies are practical ways to address the social-emotional needs of students, but they are often overlooked because teachers don't understand how to use those strategies comfortably. The following sections explain each strategy to give you a better understanding of how practical they are to implement in your everyday classroom practice and interactions.

Actively Listen to Students

In a culture where we focus on being heard versus listening to understand the viewpoint of others, the way we as educators model active listening while vali-dating our students' feelings is an effective and practical way to embed SEL in the classroom. Actively listening to our students gives us the information we need to ask them additional questions that may lead to a better understanding of their thoughts and feelings. Educators and authors Grant Chandler and Kathleen Budge (2023) write about the importance of community in the classroom and how the questions educators ask help us co-create with our students an environ-ment that fosters safety, belonging, and, ultimately, the type of community our students need to thrive as successful learners.

Active listening is defined as fully attuning to the feelings and views of the speaker, demonstrating unbiased acceptance and validation of their experience (Nelson-Jones, 2014). Active listening has three components:

1. **Listen for total meaning:** Listening for total meaning means actively listening to the speaker to grasp an understanding of what they are saying, taking note of their tone, words, and body language. This type of listening requires the listener to take an open-minded, empathetic approach while sidelining their judgment to fully understand the speaker.

2. **Respond to feelings:** When you respond to the speaker's feelings, you acknowledge the emotions behind the feelings. You are aware of their emotional state during the conversation while actively trying to understand and validate their emotions.

3. **Note all cues:** Be mindful of any shifts in language, tone of voice, or body language as the speaker is speaking, which gives you an indication of how to respond. Your response should be guided by the cues of the speaker and should provide comfort, safety, and a way to de-escalate an emotionally charged conversation (Viezzer, 2023). For example, if you notice your student is getting increasingly agitated as they are explaining a situation, you shouldn't match their tone of voice or volume. Instead, you should remain calm and speak in a lower tone to avoid further escalating the student's emotional state.

Active listening allows you to respond to the speaker in a way that conveys you heard what they said beyond how it made you feel. This helps to not only validate the speaker but also create a sense of safety which improves the overall communication in the classroom. This type of environment models the communication skills our students may need to learn, such as listening to others, understanding their feelings, and how to respond when there are differences in opinion.

Students who come to us from resource-limited socioeconomic environments have a thirty-million-word deficit compared to students from wealthier backgrounds, which impacts their overall ability to communicate (Hogenboom, 2019). This deficit equates to students not having the vocabulary necessary to express their feelings. They also may not possess the skill of listening, as they have likely had fewer conversations during their formative years. Evidence has determined the importance of reciprocal conversations among parents and their young children (Hogenboom, 2019). It's not that young children should be exposed to more vocabulary—rather, they should be using the vocabulary in conversation so they can learn not only the meaning of those words, but also the nuances of the back-and-forth conversation, sometimes referred to as a *conversation duet* (Hogenboom, 2019). This back-and-forth interaction not only develops their communication skills, but also addresses the skill of actively listening to the person speaking.

To address the SEL competencies, sometimes the simple act of modeling the behavior you would like to see goes further than any activity, reward, or gift you could present to your students. The feeling of being respected and validated by an authority figure goes a long way for our students. Being respected and validated helps build trust and strengthen the teacher-student relationship while contributing to an overall positive classroom environment. As mentioned previously, simply taking the time to get to know your students gives them an opportunity to share their thinking and feel as if they are an important part of the classroom. It also provides you with information to use when planning your instruction to ensure students see themselves in the content. When you do that, you are leveraging "relational pedagogy, which is a collection of practices and policies that leverage relationships (teacher-student and student-student) to foster learning, make meaning, and build confidence" (Hinsdale, 2016 as cited in Reibel, 2023, p. 14).

Practice Empathy and Validate Students' Feelings

Students can learn to better regulate their own behavior and emotions in an environment where empathy is modeled by the educator in the room. We can't assume our students understand or even recognize when they need to take a moment to pause, check their emotions, and determine how they will respond to others—even if that person is the teacher in the room. Nor do we want to get into a power struggle with an angry student who probably shut down moments prior and has stopped listening to what we have to say. It may seem difficult to not engage a student in a shouting match, but no one wins in such an altercation.

As I discussed in chapter 1 (page 9), many of our students come to school each day with a myriad of emotions they are not always sure how to navigate or manage. So, when they are triggered, they don't have the skills to manage or control their response. In the classroom and throughout the school day, teachers encounter those emotions and must intentionally respond empathetically to students, being mindful of their emotional cues. The teacher's response can further establish or destroy the teacher-student relationship (Aldrup, Carstensen, & Klusmann, 2022).

One of the issues highlighted during the early stages of the COVID-19 pandemic was that students battled social isolation and anxiety. Of the students surveyed in a research study at Lesley University, 43 percent reported higher levels of loneliness, and fewer than half of those students felt school provided enough support or guidance on how to make responsible decisions, handle conflicts, or manage their emotions (Lesley University, n.d.). Students are aware that they need these basic life skills, and they want to learn those skills in their schools and classrooms. Unfortunately, with the increase of innovative technology, students spend more time on computers, phones, and social media than they spend engaged in meaningful conversations and making connections with peers and adults, which is detrimental to the development of those skills (Ruyle, Child, & Dome, 2022).

Take a moment and think about your immediate response when students display behavior that is not in line with your expectations. Is giving consequences your first response, or do you try to understand what triggered the student and why they can't manage their response and emotions? Often, we try to manage the student's behavior and discourage future infractions by giving an "appropriate" consequence, but does that address the root cause of the behavior? When we foster an environment that leads with empathy, we first try to understand and are sensitive to the realities of another without using punitive measures to shift behavior. Rather, we aim to develop a connection with students that allows them to recognize their own emotional shifts so they can manage and regulate their behavior.

One way for teachers to foster this type of environment is to validate the feelings and emotions that students may be experiencing. This type of acknowledgment is not the same as validating the behavior, but it allows the student to be seen and heard, which is what the behavior may be unconsciously trying to elicit (Jung, 2023). If we want our students to operate under an empathy lens, we must also operate under that same lens, and validating our students' feelings and emotions during a time of high stress is the perfect example of empathy. How we respond to our students sets the standard for how students treat each other, which determines how emotionally safe students feel in the classroom.

Following are a few examples of things to say that acknowledge your students' feelings and can help them process and regulate their emotions.

- ► "I see that [situation or event] bothered you. Is there anything I can do to help you work through it?"

- ► "It appears your body language is changing. Is there something you'd like to discuss?"

- ► "I understand this situation may be difficult for you right now. How can I support you?"

- ► "I appreciate you expressing how you feel in this moment. How can I help you address this situation?"

- ► "I hear you, and your feelings are valid. Do you need to take a moment to pause and take a few deep breaths before we continue?"

We may not think of showing empathy in the classroom as a practical strategy to address our students' social-emotional needs, but indeed it is. As we see challenges in our students' behavior and emotional regulation, teachers recognize that they must teach and lead with empathy to create an environment that feels inclusive, safe, and supportive (Lesley University, n.d.). The essence of an inclusive and safe classroom goes beyond the curriculum, and it encompasses genuine teacher-student relationships with empathy as the foundation. Taking time to reflect on your teaching practices and recognizing when adjustments may be necessary further promotes belonging, safety, and trust within your classroom. It is in environments where empathy is prevalent that students truly thrive.

Following are four questions to reflect on as you continue to cultivate a safe and inclusive environment that is developed through the lens of empathy.

In what ways do you make an effort to understand students' perspectives?

_____
_____
_____
_____
_____
_____
_____
_____
_____

In what ways do you validate your student's feelings?

_____
_____
_____
_____
_____
_____
_____
_____
_____

Do your students feel you're approachable? Do they feel comfortable asking you questions or for help? How might you improve in this area?

_____
_____
_____
_____
_____
_____
_____
_____

INTENTIONAL

MEANINGFUL

PRACTICAL

AUTHENTIC

CONSISTENT

TEAMWORK

Do you act out of proactive concern? Are you able to detect when the energy shifts within the classroom and offer support before situations arise?

_____

_____

_____

_____

_____

_____

_____

_____

_____

After taking some time to reflect on these questions, evaluate your current practice when it comes to handling high-stress moments in the classroom. Are there opportunities for you to shift how you interact with emotionally charged students? Do your actions add additional fuel to an already hot flame? If so, here are a few things you can do to shift the energy in your classroom from being emotionally charged to the emotionally safe environment your students need as they work through expressing how they are feeling in a way that allows them to feel seen, heard, and valued.

▶ Create a plan of action to deal with emotionally charged behaviors inside the classroom. This keeps you from being reactive to the behaviors your students display, which may escalate the situation out of your control.

▶ Develop a code word or phrase with your students that they can use when they feel they are getting emotionally charged. This should be used in moderation so students don't take advantage of this strategy.

▶ Give students some mindfulness strategies they can practice in their seat inside the classroom that do not bring attention to a situation that has the potential to disrupt the classroom environment. This may be as simple as telling the student to close their eyes, tune out the noise, and take five quiet deep breaths to get regulated.

These strategies are simple but effective. When there is no plan in place to deal with emotionally charged behavior, we can plan to fail when we are put in unexpected situations. Addressing our students' SEL needs doesn't need to be complicated. It can be impactful, no matter how simple the strategy may be. The goal is to help students develop the skills they need to process their emotions and know how to manage them when needed.

Model Vulnerability

Brené Brown (2012) defines *vulnerability* as "uncertainty, risk, and emotional exposure" (p. 1). Emotionally exposing oneself to students is not high on teachers' to-do lists, especially when they are unsure how students would react to their teacher showing any emotion that makes them appear weak. The word vulnerability has often been equated with revealing one's authentic emotions, which could be mistaken for weakness. The last thing a teacher wants is to appear weak to a classroom full of students who might try to use weakness to their advantage.

It takes courage to be open and honest with your students, especially when sharing something you may be struggling with personally. It is that type of sharing that builds trust and connection when the classroom environment has been cultivated to handle it. Being vulnerable with your students makes you appear human. You are someone with feelings and are subject to some of the same emotions they have and mistakes they make. Students need to know that there are times when you feel sad, when you have sympathy for others when bad things happen to them, and you understand when someone may need a word of encouragement. Being vulnerable ourselves plays a part in developing our students' empathy muscles. "Underneath all the best practices and strategies and theories and high-stakes testing and educational bureaucracy remains one critical component for successful teaching: Vulnerability" (Armstrong, 2017).

Here are three ways we can foster vulnerability in our classrooms with our students.

1. **Lead by example:** Take opportunities to share personal experiences of overcoming adversity and challenges in life. Our students don't always recognize that their teacher has had to be resilient and overcome situations and circumstances just as they do. We often

appear to have it all together, so sharing past experiences allows our students to understand that we all face obstacles in life that we must overcome.

2. **Establish clear expectations:** In cultivating a classroom environment that can handle vulnerable moments from you or your students, you must establish clear expectations around student behavior. Your students need to understand the importance of treating their peers with kindness, respect, and empathy, and that disrespect won't be tolerated. For example, when you have a student who is going through a difficult time, make sure students are mindful of their classmate's feelings. This contributes to a trusting classroom environment. All students must feel safe sharing so conversations can be authentic and promote connection and community in the classroom. Before you allow students to share things that may be considered personal or sensitive information, make certain you have established the norms in the classroom for the conversation.

3. **Provide opportunities for reflection:** Incorporate regular opportunities for students to reflect on their learning in your classroom. Encourage students to take an active role by recognizing what is going well and what needs improvement, even when that improvement involves acknowledging (even if just to yourself) that your instructional practices have not proven effective with that specific student or a larger group of students. Allowing your students to provide feedback on your teaching practices to enhance their learning is vulnerability at its core.

Cultivating an atmosphere that encourages student vulnerability can have a profound effect on your students' learning experience. This type of atmosphere fosters trust and safety, two components that foster a growth mindset. Your students need to see that struggles, obstacles, and mistakes may happen in life, but they are able to overcome them if they don't give up. You are their example of resilience, so make sure you take advantage of every opportunity to model it for your students.

Connecting is the Ultimate Goal

One of my favorite quotes is from James Comer (1995), "No significant learning occurs without a significant relationship." This quote speaks volumes about the importance of connection. Note that he didn't say there would be no learning, but rather, *significant* learning. Have you ever stopped to reflect on the relationship you had with certain students and how that relationship impacted their learning? When you stop to think about that question and specific students who performed well in your class, maybe you realize it was the safety of the relationship that allowed those students to take risks and be vulnerable and transparent with their thinking. Because they trusted that your feedback and response to their thinking would not be negative but rather supportive while offering the proper guidance, they felt free to expand their thinking on the content.

When you look at Maslow's hierarchy of needs, after one's physiological and safety needs are met, the next need we have is to feel as if we are loved and belong (Mcleod, 2024). This need for belonging also encompasses the feeling of connectedness in relationships. Our students not only need to have a sense of belonging within their families, but they look for that same sense of belonging in school with their peers and teachers. While our primary goal as teachers is to educate our students, we can't discount the power of the feeling of connection that contributes to students' mental and academic well-being. The more connected our students feel, the more their ability to learn and overall experience will improve (Lesley University, n.d.).

It is important that we acknowledge the unique background and experiences of our students and how those factors affect their overall experience. Our students bring their aspirations, dreams, fears, and insecurities to our classrooms each day, and the connection they feel or don't feel can feed any one of those feelings, good or bad. It is the power of connection that helps build confidence and resilience in our students. Anindya Kundu (McKibben, 2022), a sociologist and an assistant professor of education at Florida International University, wants to dispel the myth that some students want to learn while others may not:

> One thing I try to do in my work is combat implicit deficit perspectives, the idea that some students are not as interested in learning as others. That's the place to start, to reframe that script and remind ourselves that all students, if we can just connect with them, really desire to learn and really desire to improve something in their lives. (McKibben, 2022)

As educators, we recognize that content and pedagogy are at the heart of the work we do every day; it is the bond and connection we forge with our students that help make magic. It is those bonds that provide our students with the safety they need in order to stretch their thinking and take risks while learning. Years after students leave your classroom, they may not remember every problem they had to solve, but they will remember how you made them feel every time they entered your classroom. They will remember the safety you provided, the confidence you instilled, and the unwavering belief you had in their potential to be a learner in your classroom. The power of connection is a catalyst that can transform everyday instruction into a personal and meaningful learning experience for your students.

Think about how you try to establish a feeling of connectedness in the classroom and answer the following questions.

Are there students who often seem isolated or excluded from group activities in your classroom? If so, how do you incorporate them into classroom activities so they can feel they belong?

_____
_____
_____
_____
_____
_____
_____
_____
_____

How do students resolve conflict in the classroom? Do your students display empathy when handling conflicts with their peers?

_____

_____

_____

_____

_____

_____

_____

_____

_____

How do students demonstrate they feel comfortable openly sharing their thoughts and opinions in class?

_____

_____

_____

_____

_____

_____

_____

_____

_____

Do your students react negatively when they receive constructive feedback, or do they see it as an opportunity for improvement?

_____

_____

_____

_____

_____

_____

_____

_____

_____

INTENTIONAL

MEANINGFUL

PRACTICAL

AUTHENTIC

CONSISTENT

TEAMWORK

By answering these questions, you can gauge the pulse inside the classroom and make the necessary adjustments. Creating an environment where students feel they belong is a process that may need to be adjusted as you discover more information about your students. This is not a one-size-fits-all approach to learning but an approach that adapts to the students in the classroom so you can develop a connection that inspires and motivates them to perform at their highest potential.

At the end of the chapter (page 74) is "SEL Classroom Strategies Quiz," a reproducible fifteen-question quiz for you to take to determine how often you use the strategies of actively listening, demonstrating empathy and validating students' feelings, and showing vulnerability in the classroom to address students' social-emotional needs. Then, look at the scoring rubric to see where your results landed and consider making the suggested adjustments that can help you embed active listening, empathy, validation, and vulnerability into your classroom culture.

Closing Thoughts

It is the simple acts of kindness that make the biggest difference in your students' lives. When you listen to what your students have to say, when you act as a voice of reason, and when you are transparent about the realities of life, it will mean more to your students than any tangible gift you can give them. We tend to forget that our vulnerability and ability to empathize with our students is an effective way to address their social-emotional needs while continuing to foster your relationship with them. By using a practical lens and practicing active listening, empathy, and validation, you are not just using strategies to address your students' needs, but you are modeling essential skills your students will use for a lifetime.

Chapter 3: Check Your IMPACT

1. What opportunities do I take to get to know my students, their backgrounds, and how their experiences may affect whether they trust me to prioritize their best interests?

   _____

   _____

   _____

   _____

   _____

   _____

   _____

2. How do I react when a student points out a mistake or misunderstanding I may have made?

   _____

   _____

   _____

   _____

   _____

   _____

   _____

3. How do I step out of my comfort zone to support my students?

   _____

   _____

   _____

   _____

   _____

   _____

   _____

4. How do I ensure every student's voice is heard regardless of their background or past interactions?

   _____

   _____

   _____

   _____

   _____

   _____

   _____

page 1 of 3

5. How often do I encourage students who may shy away from classroom discussions to participate?

_____

_____

_____

_____

_____

_____

_____

6. How have I fostered an atmosphere of mutual respect among my students and myself?

_____

_____

_____

_____

_____

_____

_____

7. How do I uplift and support students who display vulnerability in the classroom?

_____

_____

_____

_____

_____

_____

_____

8. In what ways do I create a classroom culture that views vulnerability and empathy as a strength instead of a weakness?

_____

_____

_____

_____

_____

_____

_____

_____

_____

page 2 of 3

9. How do I handle moments of discomfort for me and my students?

_____

_____

_____

_____

_____

_____

_____

10. Do I shy away from difficult topics or conversations so I don't have to display vulnerability?

_____

_____

_____

_____

_____

_____

_____

SEL Classroom Strategies Quiz

1. **What is active listening?**
   a. Listening to music while studying
   b. Listening attentively and actively engaging with the speaker
   c. Ignoring distractions while studying
   d. Listening to lectures without taking notes

2. **Which of the following is an example of empathy?**
   a. Ignoring students' emotions and concerns
   b. Understanding and sharing the feelings of students
   c. Focusing solely on academic performance
   d. Dismissing students' perspectives

3. **What does validation mean in the context of creating an inclusive learning environment?**
   a. Ignoring students' achievements and progress
   b. Discouraging diverse perspectives in discussions
   c. Acknowledging students' efforts and accomplishments
   d. Belittling students' opinions and ideas

4. **How can vulnerability contribute to a positive learning environment?**
   a. By avoiding personal connections with students
   b. By being open and honest about one's own mistakes or limitations
   c. By dismissing students' fears or anxieties
   d. By maintaining a strict teacher-student hierarchy

5. **How can active listening positively impact student-teacher relationships?**
   a. By disregarding students' opinions during discussions
   b. By ensuring teachers dominate conversations in the classroom
   c. By demonstrating respect, understanding, and interest in what students say
   d. By providing quick answers without considering student input

6. **Which of the following best describes empathy in relation to student needs?**

   a. Disregarding individual differences among students

   b. Prioritizing academic performance over emotional well-being

   c. Implementing a one-size-fits-all approach to teaching strategies

   d. Understanding and responding to the unique needs of each student

7. **Which action demonstrates validation in an inclusive learning environment?**

   a. Providing constructive feedback on assignments

   b. Ignoring student questions during class

   c. Praising only high-achieving students

   d. Dismissing student concerns without addressing them

8. **How can teachers promote vulnerability in the classroom?**

   a. By maintaining a strict and authoritative teaching style

   b. By avoiding personal connections with students

   c. By sharing personal stories or experiences to create a safe space for students to share their own

   d. By discouraging students from expressing their emotions or concerns

9. **What is the importance of active listening in an inclusive learning environment?**

   a. It allows teachers to ignore student perspectives and concerns

   b. It helps build trust, respect, and understanding between teachers and students

   c. It promotes a competitive atmosphere among students

   d. It encourages teachers to dominate classroom discussions

10. **Which of the following is an example of validation in an inclusive learning environment?**

    a. Recognizing and appreciating diverse perspectives among students

    b. Dismissing students' opinions during class discussions

    c. Focusing solely on academic performance without considering individual needs

    d. Belittling students' achievements and progress

page 2 of 4

11. **How does vulnerability contribute to creating an inclusive learning environment?**

    a. By promoting fear and anxiety among students

    b. By maintaining a rigid teacher-student hierarchy

    c. By discouraging personal growth and self-reflection

    d. By fostering trust, openness, and connection between teachers and students

12. **What role does empathy play in creating a positive learning environment?**

    a. It fosters understanding, compassion, and support for students' experiences

    b. It encourages teachers to prioritize academic performance over emotional well-being

    c. It disregards the diverse needs of individual learners

    d. It promotes competition among peers instead of collaboration

13. **Which action demonstrates active listening in the classroom?**

    a. Ignoring student questions during lectures

    b. Providing quick answers without considering student input

    c. Listening attentively and responding thoughtfully to what students say

    d. Disregarding student opinions during group activities

14. **How can teachers show empathy toward students in an inclusive learning environment?**

    a. By dismissing students' emotions and concerns

    b. By understanding and sharing the feelings of students

    c. By focusing solely on academic performance

    d. By ignoring individual differences among students

15. **Why is validation important in creating an inclusive learning environment?**

    a. It discourages diverse perspectives in classroom discussions

    b. It avoids addressing student concerns and questions

    c. It belittles students

    d. It acknowledges and affirms the experiences, opinions, and ideas of all students

page 3 of 4

ANSWER KEY: 1. **b**, 2. **b**, 3. **c**, 4. **b**, 5. **c**, 6. **d**, 7. **a**, 8. **c**, 9. **b**, 10. **a**, 11. **d**, 12. **a**, 13. **c**, 14. **b**, 15. **d**

LETTER VALUE: A = 5 points, B = 4 points, C = 3 points, D = 2 points

How Did You Do?

0–16 points: There is some work that needs to be done to create an environment that promotes safety and inclusivity. Begin by developing a deeper understanding of students' backgrounds, cultures, and experiences. Don't rush to respond to emotionally charged behaviors so the situation does not escalate. Intentionally use inclusive language and references so all students feel seen. Use nonverbal communication cues to signal you are listening to what is being said by your students.

17–31 points: You recognize your relationships with your students is important, and you are proactively working to ensure your students feel safe, seen, and as if they belong in your classroom. You can continue to foster a positive classroom environment by minimizing distractions in the classroom by using consistent procedures and routines. Use positive reinforcements when students are following procedures that are in place. Share appropriate personal experiences that have some relatability to your students and encourage them to share experiences when the opportunity arises. Allow your students to see your passion and excitement for your content and the joy you get teaching them.

32–44 points: Your students feel safe in your classroom. You recognize there are some things you can work and reflect on. Try the following strategies: (1) use nonverbal cues to recognize when students may need resources and support academically or emotionally, (2) acknowledge and apologize for rush judgments when handling students who are emotionally charged, and (3) continue practicing empathy by being approachable and maintaining open and welcoming body language.

44–53 points: You are doing a great job ensuring your classroom environment feels safe and inclusive. Some minor adjustments you can make are to continue to encourage students to actively participate in classroom discussions by asking follow-up questions so students can expand on their thinking. Look for opportunities for students to reflect on their life experiences and how they relate to their classroom experiences. Paraphrase student responses to demonstrate your understanding of their thinking so they feel seen and heard.

The Trusted Teacher © 2025 Solution Tree Press • SolutionTree.com
Visit **go.SolutionTree.com/SEL** to download this free reproducible.

INTENTIONAL

MEANINGFUL

PRACTICAL

AUTHENTIC

CONSISTENT

TEAMWORK

INTENTIONAL

MEANINGFUL

PRACTICAL

AUTHENTIC

CONSISTENT

TEAMWORK

Be Authentic

If I learned anything from teaching middle and high school students, it was that they value authenticity and welcome the opportunity to get to know their teachers. Because I showed up as myself each day, my students could trust that I meant what I said—whether I was giving a warning about an impending consequence or vowed to help with an issue they were having.

I wanted my students to not only see me as their teacher in the classroom but as someone they could trust to help guide them through their content as well as through the challenging times of navigating the social and emotional issues that come with adolescence. I understood from my personal experience in middle and high school that it was difficult to connect with my teachers because, while they seemed knowledgeable, they didn't seem approachable. I wanted to be a different sort of figure in my students' lives.

Spelling has never been a strength of mine. One year, I shared with my students that I kept a dictionary with me as I delivered my instruction. When I was unsure if I spelled a word correctly, I would look it up and either correct myself or validate what I wrote. My students were so surprised! They thought that because I was a teacher, I must know everything. I assured them that even I am always learning and need help sometimes. As the year progressed, I noticed my students seemed more comfortable questioning themselves and their work because I didn't try to show up as a perfect teacher with nothing to learn and no opportunities for growth.

The relationships I formed with my students played a major role in my success because I essentially learned how to be a teacher while teaching. My students extended me so much grace during my formative years, and they worked hard to meet my expectations because they didn't want to disappoint me. I was able to be honest with them when things didn't go as planned, and it helped them realize that everyone makes mistakes, even teachers.

To this day, when I run into my students who are now young adults, one of the things they mention is how I was always the coolest but strictest teacher they had. They talk about the stories I used to tell, how we celebrated birthdays, and how I didn't play around in my classroom. My students knew I meant business, but they also knew I cared about their well-being and their overall success. My authenticity played a large role in establishing positive relationships with my students.

The fourth aspect of the IMPACT Framework is *authenticity* in the classroom. Allowing your students to experience you as a person is an important aspect of developing trusting relationships. Your students recognize when they are not experiencing the real you. When you allow yourself to show up—flaws and all—you help your students recognize that everyone is unique, and that uniqueness is what helps foster authentic connections and relationships.

Authenticity Helps Foster Trust

Beyond textbooks, lesson plans, and your content knowledge, how you authentically show up each day is what makes a difference in your students' educational experience. Your authenticity is characterized by your ability to demonstrate passion, empathy, and a genuine interest in connecting with your students beyond teaching your content. Showing up authentically is not about showing up perfectly; it is actually the opposite. It is showing up unafraid to display your passion for your work, quirks, and your vulnerabilities.

In chapter 3 (page 53) we talked about vulnerability as a practical strategy to engage your students, but it is also beneficial for you to recognize that it is challenging to model authenticity without displaying your vulnerability. You won't always get it right. I've never had a student hold it against me when I took accountability for my actions. When your students see you as a real person and not just their teacher, it helps further develop trust and mutual respect.

Jennifer Osborne (2021), editor of Medium's *Educate* online magazine, writes, "Creating a connection with others requires authenticity and a sense of genuineness to foster the trust and communication required for meaningful relationships. It is no different in a classroom." When your students see you as caring, passionate, and authentic, they are more likely to take an active role in their learning. They see you as someone who is concerned about their well-being, who is concerned about their success, and who they can trust. This trust helps further develop a positive teacher-student relationship, which has an impact on student learning and achievement.

Throughout this chapter, we will hear two different teachers' perspectives on how they demonstrate authenticity in their classrooms.

Authenticity From a Teacher's Perspective

This excerpt is from S. Bell, an ESOL co-teacher in Georgia who supports high school second language learners (S. Bell, personal communication, December 5, 2023). Her need to be authentic and build relationships with her students is vital to her success. Her time with her students is limited, so she must take intentional approaches to building relationships with her students. She has identified authenticity as one of the strategies she uses to build rapport.

In my current role, I teach a series of co-taught on-level English classes that include English for speakers of other languages (ESOL) learners. I've noticed that some of my ESOL students tend to shut down when they find the work challenging. Instead of advocating for themselves or seeking help, they would simply avoid doing the work. It became clear that many students, especially language learners, might lack confidence in expressing their needs. I saw an opportunity to model the skills of asking for help and advocating for support. I made it clear to my students that not completing the assigned work is not an option, and I am there to support them through various means, such as scaffolding, providing additional resources, offering remediation, and reteaching when necessary. I emphasized that this support requires collaboration; we must work together to overcome challenges and ensure their academic success. I wanted my students to see challenges as opportunities for growth and learning rather than insurmountable obstacles.

The following excerpt is from J. Ross, a high school sports medicine teacher and head athletics trainer in West Virginia (J. Ross, personal communication, November 13, 2023). He has been in the same school district since the 2000s. J. Ross has cultivated relationships with the community in which he lives because he now encounters children of past students, college classmates, and colleagues. He recognizes that the students, parents, faculty, and staff trust him because of his authenticity and transparency.

I try to be as authentic as possible in whatever I do. I often discuss personal experiences with my students and how I would have liked to do things differently. We discuss the mistakes I have made so they can learn from them. I open up often to my students so that they will feel comfortable opening up to me. When you show how vulnerable you can be, it allows the students to let down their guard to be vulnerable as well. As with discussing things I have gone through, I often will allow my students to open up about things they are currently dealing with. This can give them a different way of looking at things because I often don't see things like my current generation of students.

INTENTIONAL

MEANINGFUL

PRACTICAL

AUTHENTIC

CONSISTENT

TEAMWORK

Can you describe a specific example of how you have demonstrated authenticity in your teaching practice?

_____

_____

_____

_____

_____

_____

_____

_____

_____

How did that impact your students' learning experience?

_____

_____

_____

_____

_____

_____

_____

_____

_____

_____

Showing up authentically may sound like a practical way to foster relationships and connection with your students, but so many teachers struggle with this concept. They often grapple with showing up as themselves and understanding how much they can and should share with their students. In her article, "How to Be More Authentic at Work," social psychologist Patricia Faison Hewlin (2020) states:

> Authenticity is not really about exuding everything and baring your soul all the time. It's about identifying what's important to you and determining how much you can integrate those values into your work life or other areas, so that you can experience life satisfaction, feel engaged, and make a positive contribution to work and society.

We develop connections through shared experiences, and those shared experiences are developed when we bring our perspectives, values, and experiences into our classroom.

As you bring your experiences into your classroom, it is important to recognize where the boundaries lie when interacting with your students. Your students may seem mature enough to handle sensitive topics and conversations, but you have to ask yourself, Are you the person they should have that conversation with? It is one thing to tell your students about your hobbies, favorite foods, music, and favorite vacation spots, but you must be mindful that the experiences you share do not cross any boundaries or appear to be too personal or inappropriate for your students. Feel free to share your corny jokes, but opt out of sharing jokes that may be more appropriate for an after-work setting with friends.

Self-Awareness Is Crucial to Authenticity

One of the competencies in the SEL Framework developed by CASEL (n.d.b) is *self-awareness*, which is the ability to understand one's own emotions, thoughts, and values and how they influence behavior across contexts. This includes how you integrate those things into your classroom instruction and environment. When your students see and recognize that you have a strong awareness of self and how that awareness allows you to interact with them in a way that is authentic and true, you are modeling what healthy self-awareness looks like in action.

In her article, "How Self-Awareness Enhances Teaching," Educational Psychologist Robin LaBarbera (2021) discusses how "self-awareness is understanding that your emotions drive your behavior and impact people (positively and negatively), and it means learning how to manage those emotions, especially when we are under pressure." As the continual call for teachers to cultivate positive relationships with students gets louder and louder in the wake of students needing to feel connected to their teachers, you may feel like you must share personal experiences with your students to show you can relate to them. You have to determine whether you should share a personal story to seem relatable or if you can provide a listening ear as guidance from a neutral place.

Here are some examples of how to authentically connect with your students on a personal level.

▸ Discuss the highlights of sporting events with your student-athletes while reminiscing about connections you may have had with your high school or college teams.

▸ Talk with your students who love the arts about their latest projects and offer a compliment or encouragement whenever possible.

▸ Compliment a student's new hairstyle, clothing, or overall style. Students often don't realize we see them until we mention it.

▸ Mention the relaxing weekend you had with family and friends and how you welcomed the opportunity to enjoy their company.

Ultimately, nurturing your self-awareness will not only enhance how you deliver your instruction, but will also create a pathway for a more authentic connection with your students, cultivating an environment where learning and personal growth can flourish.

Engaging your students in authentic conversations that allow them to get to know you beyond the classroom doesn't have to be unduly complicated, but it should be genuine and appropriate. One of my favorite ways to give my students an opportunity to get to know me and my personality is to create a BioPoem and hang it in my classroom. It is a great way to describe yourself and list a few of your favorite things and places. Figure 4.1 (page 86) is an example of a BioPoem you can use to start the year and even edit as the year progresses.

INTENTIONAL MEANINGFUL PRACTICAL AUTHENTIC CONSISTENT TEAMWORK

My BioPoem

First Name _____

Three Adjectives That Describe You _____, _____, _____

Who Enjoys _____, _____, _____

Who Dislikes _____, _____, _____

Who Would Love to Visit _____

Who Would Love to Meet _____

Who Cares Deeply About _____

Who Dreams of _____

Who Values _____

Who Graduated From _____

Who Lives In _____

Last Name _____

Figure 4.1: A get-to-know-you BioPoem.

Visit **go.SolutionTree.com/SEL** for a free reproducible version of this figure.

Following is an interview excerpt with our guest teachers about balancing structure and self-expression.

Authenticity From a Teacher's Perspective

How do you balance the need for structure and discipline in the classroom with your authentic self-expression?

S. Bell: One of my core values is freedom. I believe students thrive when they have the freedom to express themselves, explore their interests, and engage with the learning process in a way that resonates with them. However, I also recognize the significance of structure and consistency in promoting a conducive learning atmosphere. My structured personality aligns with the belief that students learn best when there is a clear framework in place. This framework includes well-defined expectations, established routines, and clear boundaries. Maintaining consistency in the classroom, not only in terms of behavior expectations but also in how I authentically express myself, contributes to a sense of stability for the students. *(S. Bell, personal communication, December 5, 2023).*

J. Ross: I think both structure and discipline go hand and hand in the classroom and in society. During my twenty years of teaching, I have learned that most students want structure and discipline, even when they fight it. They would prefer to receive knowledge on what to do and not to do. When there is no structure for what your expectations are, that's when I see lost students. That's also when more issues arise. *(J. Ross, personal communication, November 13, 2023).*

Authenticity Allows Students to Be Their True Selves

Frey and colleagues (2019) discuss how we develop our self-concept and beliefs about our identity based on our interactions with others and how those interactions help fuel the narratives we tell ourselves, whether positive or negative. This includes your students. Their interactions with you will help fuel and determine the narrative they spin about themselves, especially when it comes to how they see themselves as students. When we relate this to the competency of self-awareness, our students will develop that awareness of self through interactions with their peers, family, and their teachers. This awareness will shape the stories they tell themselves about their potential, ability as a learner, and their worthiness.

The narratives our students develop often mirror the interactions they have with you, their teacher. They will consider the words you say and your actions toward them to create that narrative, but they will also consider how you show up to class each day. Can they count on you to encourage them to be resilient and persevere when things seem challenging, or do you feed into the narrative that they don't have the skills needed to be successful in your class?

You hold a unique influence in your classroom. Your students watch your every move and listen to what you say even when you think they are not paying attention. You are an example of resilience, perseverance, and accepting challenges as opportunities for growth. As you continue to be transparent and model continuous learning, your students will mimic that behavior. They will see the challenges they face in the classroom as learning opportunities.

Following are our guest teachers' sentiments on helping students feel safe to be authentic in the classroom.

Authenticity From a Teacher's Perspective

How do you foster a classroom environment where students feel safe to be themselves and express their thoughts and ideas openly?

S. Bell: In my classroom, I prioritize being approachable and genuinely interested in students' lives and well-being. Clear expectations and boundaries are established, ensuring that students understand my behavioral standards. Encouraging open communication is another priority, fostering a culture where questions and discussions are welcomed. Actively listening to students' concerns and opinions and emphasizing the value of constructive feedback helps create a supportive atmosphere. Modeling inclusivity and openness is a cornerstone of my teaching approach. I exemplify the behavior I expect from my students, demonstrate openness to different perspectives and ideas, and actively acknowledge and learn from my own mistakes, fostering a culture of continuous improvement *(S. Bell, personal communication, December 5, 2023)*.

J. Ross: When it comes to my classroom environment, the word is *family*! On the very first day of class, I express that this is not my classroom; it's our family. And just like any family, we will have both good and bad moments, but we will work through them together. I want my students to lean on each other and always try to be there for someone else because you never know when you will be the one in need.

Because of the family atmosphere, my students seem to feel safer expressing themselves. My father was a lifelong educator. At the beginning of my teaching career, he told me: "You are not a health teacher or a

> sports medicine teacher; you are a *teacher*! Make sure you never forget that you are teaching students about all aspects of life, not just your subject matter."
>
> That has stuck with me to this day. I try to attend and support students' activities at the school, like speech, debate, band, choir performances, ROTC competitions, parades, and sports games, and I stay long enough to be able to give a compliment the next day. This lets my students know I was there and I care about them beyond the classroom. I also compliment students on their shoes, outfits, hairstyle changes, grade improvements, sports performances, and so on because this shows them I care about them as people and not just as my students. *(J. Ross, personal communication, November 13, 2023).*

Your students will develop a healthy self-awareness in environments where they feel seen, heard, and valued. This type of environment is fostered through open communication coupled with constructive, nonjudgmental feedback. The hope is that our students see the challenges they face, whether academic or social, as opportunities for growth in those areas.

By nurturing positive narratives and relationships through our shared experiences, we help our students build the confidence and resilience necessary to be successful academically, but also in life in general. Let's explore a little more deeply the idea that you're not "just a teacher" and how your authenticity with students enhances peer-to-peer collaboration.

You're Not Just a Teacher

Your value as the teacher in your classroom goes beyond the content you teach. As J. Ross's father reminded him, he was not just his students' content teacher. His role as their teacher encompassed more than just teaching the curriculum. Being your students' teacher also means you equip them with skills they may use in your classroom but that also have value in the world around them. Without authenticity, transparency, and vulnerability, you pose the risk of not cultivating

INTENTIONAL   MEANINGFUL   PRACTICAL   AUTHENTIC   CONSISTENT   TEAMWORK

the type of teacher-student relationship that allows for open and honest communication. As Frey and colleagues (2019) write:

> We can't demand that students form healthy relationships with peers if we don't ourselves demonstrate the value of respect and regard we hold for our own students. Students look to us for guidance in how in-school relationships should be formed. (p. 96).

This type of communication welcomes students' voices and allows them to express their thoughts about their content and life in general. Such a learning environment is rooted in humility and listening, often requiring teachers to decenter themselves as the primary source of knowledge in the room (Safir, 2023). As you help students develop their voices and how they see themselves and the world around them, also allow for an exchange of perspectives, learning how your students perceive and experience the world, while also sharing your own position. It's not about seeing who is right or wrong, but rather understanding how one thinks, which is how you allow your students to see you as human and not just their teacher.

In your students' minds, you don't think about anything other than the subject you teach until you allow them to get to know you and how you see yourself and the world around you. They may not know that your opinion is not like the talking heads they see and hear on the news, internet, or social media because, in their mind, most adults think the same. They forget you were not always a teacher and may not realize you too were once a teenager trying to navigate life.

Finding an opportunity to include personal stories that relate to your students and content helps them learn more about you, your perspectives, and your connection to the content you teach. The stories don't have to be so personal that you feel uncomfortable telling them, but they should have some sort of connection so your students understand the point of the story. How can you talk with your students about overcoming adversity? The importance of managing their time? The value of friendship?

There are so many experiences you have had that could make an impact on how your students connect with you as their teacher. That connection is what helps fuel your relationship with them while providing them the opportunity to connect with you and their peers.

Student-to-Student Relationships

Although we tend to focus on the importance of the teacher-student relationship, we shouldn't forget or ignore the value of the student-student relationship, which is fostered when we allow our students to have a more active and vocal role in our classrooms. You should take an intentional approach when it comes to using your relatable stories to fuel opportunities for your students to share their thoughts and perspectives in class. As Amori Yee Mikami, Erik A. Ruzek, Christopher A. Hafen, Anne Gregory, and Joseph P. Allen (2017) write:

> **A study of nearly 1,100 middle and high school students in sixty-five schools found that peer relatedness was stronger in classrooms where helping behaviors were valued, and where students had the opportunity to interact academically with one another.**

Here are some ways you can foster relationships in your classroom through peer collaboration.

▸ Create an escape room challenge using your content that requires students to work together to "escape." Students are required to answer a variety of questions that consider a variety of reasoning and problem-solving strategies.

▸ Design a group project that includes a group and individual component. Students are required to complete their individual component that contributes to the overall group project but allows each person some individual responsibility and creativity.

► Play *two truths and a lie* periodically to begin class. Let chosen students know ahead of time that they will be sharing two truths and a lie with their classmates. It is up to the class to determine which statement is a lie through a process of elimination. Once the class has figured out the lie, the student has the opportunity to share briefly about their truths.

Following are some words from our guest teachers about meeting classroom challenges.

Authenticity From a Teacher's Perspective

When faced with challenges or setbacks in your teaching, how do you approach these situations authentically, and what strategies do you use to overcome them?

S. Bell: A fundamental strategy I employ is reflection, including a thoughtful examination of my teaching practices. I take the time to analyze the situation, pinpoint the root causes of the challenge, and assess my own role in it. Another valuable strategy is to seek feedback and collective wisdom from colleagues or mentors. Professional development remains an ongoing priority for me. Actively seeking out workshops, courses, or conferences equips me with new tools and strategies to overcome challenges effectively. Maintaining a positive mindset is crucial during challenging times. I strive to focus on progress and successes, no matter how small, rather than being overwhelmed by setbacks. This positive outlook not only influences my own resilience but also sets a constructive tone for the classroom environment *(S. Bell personal communication, December 5, 2023).*

J. Ross: Something I have learned is that there will be challenges to overcome every day! The key strategy that works for me is *patience*! Stand back, take a deep breath, and deal with your daily challenges one at a time. Try not to be overwhelmed by more than one thing, and don't be afraid to ask for help. So many times, we are afraid to show others that we need help. I feel as if we all need help at some point, so don't be afraid to ask for it *(J. Ross, personal communication, November 13, 2023).*

Educator Shane Safir (2023) discusses how teachers can prioritize the need for students to be active participants in their learning such that they increase their knowledge about issues that matter to them. This happens when a teacher abandons some of the traditional practices of teaching and embraces an approach that allows students to take a more collaborative approach to learning with their teachers and peers. Safir (2023) writes, "A pedagogy of voice orients us to create learning experiences that foster connection, cognitive growth, and student agency, which we define in the Street Data (formative and performance based assessments) through the domains of identity, belonging, mastery, and efficacy."

As you may notice, a pedagogy of voice requires you to cultivate an environment of shared experiences that is embedded in authentic conversations and interactions between teacher-student and student-student. It begins with recognizing that students learn best in collaborative environments where they feel safe, seen, and heard and where they can see the relevance of their content and how it fits in the world around them. Your authenticity and genuine interest in your students' social, emotional, and academic success help to foster the type of environment in which your students feel safe enough to take risks with their thinking and learning.

Figure 4.2 (page 94) is an authenticity inventory questionnaire that allows for reflection in nine areas where you can display authenticity in the classroom. Take some time to read the questions and rate yourself on a scale of 1 to 5, with 1 being, "Needs Improvement," and 5 being, "Consistently Demonstrates." After completing the questionnaire, identify the areas where you excel and the areas you would like to grow.

INTENTIONAL

MEANINGFUL

PRACTICAL

AUTHENTIC

CONSISTENT

TEAMWORK

Authenticity Inventory Questionnaire		
Authenticity Indicator	**Reflection Questions**	**Rating**
Passion	Do I genuinely love teaching and my subject matter?	1—2—3—4—5
Transparency	Am I honest about my own learning journey and willing to share my challenges and mistakes with my students?	1—2—3—4—5
Empathy	Do I make an effort to understand and relate to my students' feelings?	1—2—3—4—5
Flexibility	Am I open to adjusting my teaching methods based on my students' needs and feedback?	1—2—3—4—5
Consistency	Do I strive to consistently be authentic versus changing my personality based on the activities of the day?	1—2—3—4—5
Openness to Student Input	Do I value my students' opinions of the classroom environment and culture?	1—2—3—4—5
Respect for Individuality	Do I value my students' unique abilities and recognize their strengths and weaknesses?	1—2—3—4—5
Creating a Safe Space	Have I fostered a classroom environment where students feel safe to be themselves and express their unique opinions?	1—2—3—4—5
Reflective Practice	Do I reflect on my teaching practices and make adjustments to better align with my teaching goals?	1—2—3—4—5

Figure 4.2: Authenticity questionnaire.

*Visit **go.SolutionTree.com/SEL** for a free reproducible version of this figure.*

After filling out the authenticity questionnaire, identify the areas that are your strengths and areas where you would like to see growth. Once you have identified those areas, answer the following questions.

Which indicator had the highest rating?

As you reflect on your answer, what behaviors or actions do you think contribute most to that highest indicator rating?

Which indicator would you like to improve?

What goal can you set for yourself based on your inventory ratings?

INTENTIONAL

MEANINGFUL

PRACTICAL

AUTHENTIC

CONSISTENT

TEAMWORK

Based on your goal, create an action plan below:

Action Plan:

_____
_____
_____
_____
_____
_____
_____
_____
_____
_____

How will you measure progress?

_____
_____
_____
_____
_____
_____
_____
_____
_____
_____

How will you determine success?

_____
_____
_____
_____
_____
_____
_____
_____
_____
_____

INTENTIONAL   MEANINGFUL   PRACTICAL   AUTHENTIC   CONSISTENT   TEAMWORK

Closing Thoughts

Authenticity in the classroom goes beyond pedagogy; it is about creating a space where students can show up as their authentic selves and feel seen and valued. As educators, our job entails more than just imparting content knowledge; it also requires us to foster an environment of mutual respect and understanding. Your authenticity is the cornerstone of meaningful educational experiences where students are encouraged to be active participants in their learning. We are all looking for a true sense of connection and belonging, and the reciprocal exchange of experiences and perspectives between teachers and students is one piece of the puzzle that fosters that belonging.

INTENTIONAL

MEANINGFUL

PRACTICAL

AUTHENTIC

CONSISTENT

TEAMWORK

Chapter 4: Check Your IMPACT

1. In what ways can I show up authentically in the classroom and make a positive impact on my students' lives?

_____

_____

_____

_____

_____

_____

_____

2. How do I convey to my students that I care about their success academically and socially?

_____

_____

_____

_____

_____

_____

_____

3. How do I foster a classroom culture where students feel safe to express themselves without fear of being judged or ridiculed by peers?

_____

_____

_____

_____

_____

_____

_____

4. Do I take time to reflect on my teaching practices and how they align with my career goals?

_____

_____

_____

_____

_____

_____

_____

5. Do I feel comfortable discussing my learning journey with my students, including my successes and failures?

_____

_____

_____

_____

_____

_____

_____

6. Am I consistent with my actions and behavior toward my students, or do my actions shift depending on the circumstances and situations?

_____

_____

_____

_____

_____

_____

_____

7. How do I offer support to students who may be struggling academically or socially?

_____

_____

_____

_____

_____

_____

_____

8. Do I create opportunities for students to share their thoughts and experiences with the class? When they share, am I genuinely interested in their contributions?

_____

_____

_____

_____

_____

_____

_____

9. How do I ensure I'm approachable enough for my students to feel they can offer suggestions about what I am teaching?

    _____

    _____

    _____

    _____

    _____

    _____

    _____

10. How do I handle moments when I make a mistake or when I can't answer student questions?

    _____

    _____

    _____

    _____

    _____

    _____

    _____

Remain Consistent

As I mentioned in the introduction (page 1), I never intended to become a teacher, but because of an unexpected job loss, I found myself filling a vacant seventh-grade English teacher position. This was in mid-October of 2006, and the position had been open since August. Initially, I was excited because I had been a substitute teacher throughout college, and I truly enjoyed the experience. However, I quickly had a reality check because I was my students' sixth teacher in six weeks. I was also their teacher for the rest of the year, the only one who decided to stay and provide the students with some consistency.

I admit, it was hard! I went in thinking I could simply give the students some directions, and they would follow them without question. What I didn't realize was that seventh-grade students didn't take well to someone they didn't know barking orders at them. So, my thinking about how I would run my classroom quickly changed. I assumed my students would come into the classroom and take a seat, but of course, that didn't happen. They would gather and visit each other, and it took at least five minutes for me to establish any order. They would walk around to sharpen pencils and throw away paper in the middle of instruction, which would disrupt any hard-won engagement I had during that moment. I knew I wanted my students to be successful learners despite my lack of formal training, and I was determined to figure out what that looked like. I watched my students have appropriate behavior in other classes, so I knew they were capable! But I was missing something.

I observed in awe how my veteran teammate ran her classroom. Her students were always orderly, engaged, and seldom got out of line. She had great relationships with her students, and they didn't mind following her rules or adhering to the procedures she had implemented to run her classroom. I was determined not only to develop relationships with my students, but to have a classroom that ran like my teammate's class.

One month after filling that position, I was able to attend my first professional development training. It focused on the importance of creating rules, procedures, and routines in the classroom. This professional development was a blessing, especially since the facilitator visited each participant's classroom four weeks after the training to give feedback on how we had implemented the learning. It made me realize that I had skipped one of the most important steps in creating a positive classroom environment: implementing the procedures and routines that allow my students to be engaged but independent learners.

The following week, I did a reset in my classroom. It is never too late to do a reset of your classroom if things are not going as you envisioned. I told my students there would be some changes to classroom routines and procedures. At times, I wanted to abandon the mission, but I stayed consistent in holding my students accountable. I am happy to report that by January my students had come to appreciate the structure in the classroom.

After that rocky first year of teaching, I became a firm believer that it was easier to loosen up than tighten up. I began taking the first four weeks of school as an opportunity not only to introduce myself to my students, but also introduce them to the procedures and routines they would need to be successful learners in my classroom. Even though I introduced the procedures my students needed to enter school and my classroom on the first day of school, I had to consistently remind them what was expected until the procedure turned into a routine for them. Over the course of the next few weeks, I clearly explained, modeled, and adjusted my procedures based on the needs of my students and the climate I wanted to create.

Properly implementing the necessary procedures and routines takes time and consistency, especially when it seems that things are not going as planned. As educators, we may feel that students in higher grades don't need as much structure as students in lower grades, as it may hinder their participation in class. However, students welcome structure and consistency because it helps them understand how they can be successful. Once I became consistent with enforcing my procedures, my students began to adjust their behavior.

This chapter focuses on the importance of *consistency* in our practice and how the implementation of procedures and routines is an important aspect of this. "When students experience consistent and predictable routines, it contributes to the safety that drives engagement in learning" (Stafford-Brizard, 2024, p. 24). As you read through this chapter, take some time to think about the procedures you have in your classroom. Do you enforce them consistently, or are they only enforced when things get a little chaotic? Are you hesitant in creating procedures because of the age of your students, or do you welcome the opportunity to help your students self-manage their behaviors due to the structure in your classroom? Be open to opportunities to revamp some of your procedures and routines to support the overall environment in your classroom.

Consistency Fosters Safety

A lack of structure and consistent procedures embedded into the classroom routine lends itself to inefficient transitions, off-task behavior, and students needing to ask a variety of questions, resulting in less time for teaching and learning. It may not appear that these things are connected to our students' social-emotional needs, but, in reality, they are. As we discussed in chapter 1, CASEL (n.d.b) notes that for students to participate fully and respectfully in a relationship-centered environment, they must possess basic social-emotional skills. CASEL (n.d.b) also notes that positive learning environments have the teacher-student relationship at the center. These learning environments are well-managed, participatory, and hold students to high expectations. These environments use instructional and classroom management strategies to address students' social-emotional needs and are motivating and psychologically and physically safe.

"I don't have time to implement SEL practices into my school day." This is what some educators tell me when the conversation around SEL and relationships enters the picture. They like to tell me how they must get through their pacing guide along with all their instructional content, and SEL practices are just one more thing they don't have time to worry about or focus on.

This is when it's important to remember a lesson from chapter 4 (page 79). You're not *just* a content teacher. As educators, we are charged not only with teaching our students instructional content, but also how to interact within the social aspects of the school day. Behavior skills are no different from academic skills in that they represent acquired learning, not innate knowledge (Buffum et al., 2024). When teachers create and implement effective routines and procedures, they help students feel safe, supported, and engaged, which can, in turn, support their social-emotional well-being. These supports are embedded in the environment, which helps students manage themselves by reinforcing expectations and promoting positive behavior even when the teacher is unavailable (Jones, McGarrah, & Kahn, 2019).

Our consistency in implementing effective procedures and routines communicates to our students that we care about them, their well-being, and their education. This consistency helps create a safe classroom environment that is conducive to student learning. Jones and Bouffard (2012, as cited in Bailey, Stickle, Brion-Meisels, & Jones, 2019) note that key social-emotional skills include focusing, listening attentively, following directions, managing emotions, dealing with conflicts, and working cooperatively with peers. Correlational studies show that classrooms function more effectively and student learning increases when children can focus their attention, manage negative emotions, navigate relationships with peers and adults, and persist in the face of difficulty (Osher et al., 2016; Jones et al., 2019).

Effective classroom routines and procedures can help address students' social-emotional needs in a variety of ways. Clear guidelines for communication and problem solving can help students develop social skills and feel empowered to resolve conflicts. Procedures for managing disruptions and behavior issues can help students feel safe and secure in the classroom while reducing stress and anxiety. The feeling of safety, support, and connectedness to the classroom environment directly correlates to student engagement and academic success. As National University (n.d.) notes, "As a student is provided the tools associated with SEL, they will have more ownership of their actions, a sense of belonging, and will intrinsically care about their education." In short, effective classroom procedures and routines create a safe and predictable environment that promotes positive relationships, emotional regulation, and peer collaboration.

What routines and procedures do you implement at the beginning of the school year?

_____
_____
_____
_____
_____
_____
_____
_____
_____

How do those routines and procedures support your students' independence in the classroom?

_____
_____
_____
_____
_____
_____
_____
_____
_____

Establish Routines in the First Four Weeks of School

As I progressed in my career, establishing procedures and routines became the focus of the start of the school year. I realized I couldn't forget about my content, but I also knew that how I taught my students how to operate in the classroom was essential to their success. So, I took the first twenty days of school to review the prior year's skills while teaching my students classroom procedures and routines. Because I taught reading, there were quite a few diagnostic tests and assessments my students had to take in order to be placed in their reading and intervention groups. That provided me the perfect opportunity to spiral in some content while teaching my students the essential procedures and routines.

The following is a weekly breakdown of how you can implement routines in the first twenty days (or four weeks) of the school year.

Week One

As we know, the first week of school is filled with a lot of uncertainty and chaos. We are meeting our students and parents for the first time. The students we begin with on the first day of school may not be the same students we end up with because students come and go, schedules change, and there may be teacher vacancies that can impact everyone in the school. Despite this chaos, we still need to have a plan in place for the students in our classroom. Think of meeting your students for the first time as you thought about meeting your administrator. Your students and some parents will immediately begin to form opinions of how your classroom will operate based on your short time together.

During this first week, focus on getting to know your students as individuals. I focused a lot of my attention on tasks students would complete independently. The tasks assigned would allow me to teach the procedures the students would need inside and outside of the classroom, even if I was absent for the day. The focus this week should be to ensure that students know what is expected of them as learners, how they can be successful, and for what they will be held accountable. Since I taught middle reading, the assignments given during the first five days were short in nature but allowed me to assess my students' writing skills, how well they followed written directions, and their critical thinking skills using text. Some of their tasks might be:

▸ Writing and illustrating a BioPoem about themselves to be displayed during the school open house

▸ Engaging in scavenger hunts to become familiar with key areas inside the classroom

▸ Completing classroom activities where students provide quick short answers; activities such as passing a ball around the room, and the student holding it when the music stops has to answer a question. Or, the name game, where everyone learns each other's name by saying their name and repeating everyone's name who went before them. Although this is an individual task, it functioned as a teambuilding exercise since students were getting to know each other.

▸ Completing a short writing prompt describing their ideal day at school; students could also describe their ideal day in your classroom. This would give you an idea of the type of tasks you could plan as the year progresses.

▸ Completing a do-now opening assignment; these are assigned by day three for students to complete at the beginning of class. This is one of the first procedures students learn to help them transition to the beginning of class. You may want to think about including this or another procedure that can help students transition into your classroom. This procedure will eventually turn into a routine that students will do without prompting if it is consistently enforced.

Because this first week is about getting to know your students, their personalities, and how well they interact with classmates naturally, there will be less of a focus on building student-student relationships. The following weeks will focus on working with classmates and creating a sense of belonging. Use this week to get to know your students and allow them to get to know you and your expectations in the classroom. This is also a great time to teach specific procedures that will eventually be the routines that allow the classroom to operate as a well-oiled machine.

Here are some of the procedures to focus on during the first five days of school. Since there are so many aspects that run off procedures, this is not a

INTENTIONAL

MEANINGFUL

PRACTICAL

AUTHENTIC

CONSISTENT

TEAMWORK

complete list, but the following should give you a good idea of the procedures you might create for your classroom to run smoothly and efficiently.

- ▶ How and where to enter the school each day
- ▶ What to do if you are or are not eating breakfast each morning
- ▶ How and where to enter the grade-level hallway
- ▶ Behavior expected in the hallway and at lockers
- ▶ How and when to enter the classroom
- ▶ How to get materials needed to begin the day
- ▶ How to submit homework, signed paperwork, and communications from parents
- ▶ What to do if you complete your assignment early
- ▶ What to do in case of emergency
- ▶ How to gather extra supplies

The first week of school may be filled with uncertainty and chaos, but it is crucial that you take the time to get to know your students as individuals while setting the foundation for a successful school year. By teaching your students the classroom procedures, you set the stage for a well-organized and structured learning environment that your students will learn to appreciate and value.

How do you ensure your students understand the purpose of your procedures at the beginning of the school year?

_____

_____

_____

_____

_____

_____

_____

_____

_____

How do you know when you need to adjust classroom procedures?

_____

_____

_____

_____

_____

_____

_____

_____

_____

_____

Week Two

As the dust begins to settle from the chaotic first week of school, use week two to build the culture and climate within your classroom by fostering student-to-student relationships. We talk a lot about the teacher-student relationship but not enough about the student-student relationship. Even though students spend a lot of their time with us, they spend just as much time with their classmates and must work with their classmates in a variety of settings.

This week is designed so students are paired with other classmates throughout the week. They are not necessarily partnered with the same person each day. Switching partners allows you to get a sense of who can and cannot work together for a variety of reasons—whether it is because of personalities clashing, the partners are too social or too quiet, or because they are both indecisive and nothing gets accomplished.

This week, plan to focus on tasks that must be completed with a partner. Some of the tasks can be completed during the class period and some can carry over. You only have five days, so be mindful about the task because you will move into a different format the following week. Following are some examples of tasks you might assign.

> ▸ Conduct an interview of your partner and introduce them to another pair of students. Be creative with this task. How could you incorporate your content into this task? Could your students be an equation that

their classmates have to solve? Can they be a famous scientist? What about important figures from history?

▶ Partner reading incorporates the jigsaw method, which is where each student reads a specific portion of text and is responsible for explaining the information to their partner. Once they have finished reading, they can complete a skill-focused graphic organizer.

▶ Have students complete a content-focused scavenger hunt as a pair. This scavenger hunt can be focused on reviewing past skills or used to introduce an upcoming unit.

This week should have a heavy focus on how the members of your classroom community treat each other, with a very intentional focus on collaboration and conflict-resolution skills. Students don't get to change partners just because they have a disagreement. As you may notice, the example tasks assigned are not content-heavy in nature but are more focused on the skill of collaborating with a classmate. If you are ready to tackle content-rich tasks, you can begin with reviewing needed content knowledge from the previous years to assess your students' prior knowledge for upcoming instruction. This could be as simple as turning your scavenger hunt into an activity that focuses on using your textbook and relevant websites to look up information for an upcoming unit. You may even create an escape game using content that consists of clues that build off each other to solve. To increase the collaboration, have a prize for the group that escapes first and can explain their strategy. You may need to do a lot of procedure front-loading and stopping students to give reminders or help them work through minor conflicts.

Recognize that students not only go to school to learn, but they also go to see friends and socialize. My classroom was never a quiet one, but I am a firm believer in "organized chaos," and I believe it's imperative to introduce, practice, and adjust the procedures you teach during this week. Along with the procedures students learned the previous week, introduce students to the following.

▶ How to transition into partner work

▶ How to find space to work when partners are in different areas of the classroom

- ▶ What it looks like or means to work as partners

- ▶ How and who gathers needed materials

- ▶ What the expected volume is while working with a classmate

- ▶ How to store assignments that have not been completed

- ▶ How to turn in completed work

- ▶ How to get replacement materials

- ▶ How to transition back to your individual seat

- ▶ How to ask for help

By focusing on cultivating the student-student relationship, students will be able to practice collaboration, communication, and conflict-resolution skills that are important for success in school and beyond. By establishing clear procedures for partner work, students should be able to work efficiently and effectively while maintaining a positive social atmosphere in the classroom. Through intentional pairing and carefully designed tasks, students should be able to work with and navigate the various personalities in the classroom. It is important to note that week two procedures build upon the procedures taught during week one, so make sure you maintain a list of the procedures you teach so you can reinforce them consistently.

How do you normally handle partner work in your classroom?

_____

_____

_____

_____

_____

_____

_____

_____

_____

_____

INTENTIONAL | MEANINGFUL | PRACTICAL | AUTHENTIC | CONSISTENT | TEAMWORK

How do you adjust your expectations when student pairs are not working out?

_____

_____

_____

_____

_____

_____

_____

_____

_____

Week Three

As students begin to get comfortable with their classmates, it is important to foster positive relationships among them to create a supportive learning environment where everyone feels included and valued. Although the previous week was spent pairing students with their classmates, during week three they should spend more time completing a group task. This task will continue into the next week, but we will get into that in week four.

This week focuses on team building and creating a culture of belonging. Place students in groups with a maximum of five students per group. Design the group task to require all students to work together collaboratively to achieve a common goal related to the content. This can be the first task of your opening unit. There should be a mix of instruction, group work, conferencing with students, and independent work time. This type of task works best when a rubric is used to give students an understanding of what you are expecting as a final product. As students work and learn together, they will learn how to communicate effectively while simultaneously developing trust and respect for their peers.

During this week you will not only be reinforcing the procedures from weeks one and two, but you will also be introducing the procedures needed to work in groups. Making sure to maintain your list of procedures is critical so you are consistent when it comes to the everyday aspects of your classroom. Even though students will be working with multiple classmates, the way they enter, transition, ask for help, get replacement materials, and exit the classroom should not change, so make sure students are adhering to the procedures they have been learning during this time. Don't forget you may need to remind and model the procedures multiple times before they become routine.

In my classroom, since I was a reading teacher, I had my students create a picture book that carried the theme of Teamwork Makes the Dream Work. I used a picture book titled *Five Little Fiends*, authored by Sarah Dyer (2002), as my mentor text. Students were responsible for producing their own original picture book based on the theme of teamwork. The students were to come up with the characters, setting, plot, and original illustrations for their book. Each member of the group was responsible for two pages of original content and artwork, but all pages were required to tell a cohesive story. This task ended with students putting their books together and reading them to the class. I used a rubric to grade the task, so students knew exactly what I was looking for and what they needed to do to get maximum points.

This activity allowed me to observe how well students could express their thoughts in writing, their spelling, their ability to use descriptive language, and how well they could develop a plot, which are all key components of reading and writing. This task carried over into the following week because students would need time to discuss their ideas and come to a consensus on the story. I also began to deliver mini-lessons so they could experience my instruction and what was expected of them during that time. This week gave students an authentic experience of the structure of the classroom because not only did they use content to complete this task, but they also completed their do-nows as they entered the classroom, one of their opening procedures, and exit tickets as they left, one of their closing procedures.

Although this is an example of using group work to teach additional procedures, foster team building, and introduce students to content in the reading classroom, this can be modified for any content area. See the following ideas for how you can use this framework in your content.

- ▶ **Mathematics:** Have students create a business where each member of the team is responsible for creating a product for the business. Each member will price out their product and determine the cost associated with bringing the product to market. Allow your students to market their products to their classmates to determine how much they can sell. Have students complete a profit and loss analysis to determine which business makes the most money. The group that comes away with the largest profit wins (if you want to make it a competition).

▶ **History:** Have students create a community in the geographic area or during a particular time in history, whichever is most appropriate for your area of study. Each member of the team must help create the name, the type of government, the economy, the education system, and where or how the members of the community will live. Allow students to create a model of their community to display for the class. You may even adopt the names of the communities to represent your class switching periodically to ensure all groups are acknowledged during the school year.

▶ **Science:** Your students are the world's leading scientists, and they have just been charged with naming a new species that was found in a newly explored part of the earth. Members of the group will be required to name the species, classify the species, and describe the environment in which the species was discovered. Members of the group should create a model or poster of the species in its natural habitat while explaining what the species must eat to survive. The species should be representative of the environments or type of science that your students will study during the school year.

Team-building activities are a great way to foster positive relationships and create a supportive learning environment while allowing students to put the procedures they have learned into practice. With students working together in groups, some of the procedures you may want to teach are:

▶ How to transition into and out of group activities

▶ Where to place unfinished group work

▶ How to choose group roles

▶ What to do if there is a disagreement within the group

▶ How to submit group assignments

▶ What to do if a group member is not contributing to the group task

- ▸ How to gather materials for the group

- ▸ What to do if a member of the group is absent

Ultimately, prioritizing positive relationships among students not only benefits their academic success but also helps them develop important social and emotional skills that will serve them well beyond the classroom. By creating a supportive learning environment that values collaboration, communication, and respect, teachers can help students feel empowered, engaged, and motivated to learn. As we continue to prioritize building positive relationships among students, we create a foundation for a successful and fulfilling educational journey.

Do you avoid group activities? Why do you think that might be?

_____
_____
_____
_____
_____
_____
_____
_____
_____
_____

Do you allow your students to have a voice in the classroom procedures? In what ways do you help foster a sense of ownership among your students?

_____
_____
_____
_____
_____
_____
_____
_____
_____
_____

INTENTIONAL

MEANINGFUL

PRACTICAL

AUTHENTIC

CONSISTENT

TEAMWORK

Week Four

As you approach the end of the first twenty days of school, your students begin to settle into a routine. This is the time when classroom structures and procedures become fully integrated into daily life, and students begin to function independently. Students begin to understand what is expected of them, and they start to take ownership of their own learning. This is an exciting time for both students and teachers, as it marks the beginning of a more collaborative and productive classroom environment.

One of the most important benefits of establishing clear classroom procedures and expectations is it allows students to become independent learners with the strategies necessary to manage their behavior inside of the classroom. Instead of relying on the teacher to prompt them or remind them of what to do, students can take responsibility for their own learning. Effective classroom management strategies aim to establish an environment that promotes positive learning outcomes by incorporating proactive measures to address potential disruptive behaviors, rather than relying solely on reactive approaches (Egeberg, McConney, & Price, 2016).

Another benefit of established and consistent classroom procedures is that they create a sense of predictability and stability. Students thrive on routine, and having clear expectations and procedures in place helps them feel safe and secure in the classroom environment. Teachers who have effective classroom management skills often create a predictable learning environment by implementing techniques that decrease disruptive behavior (Oliver & Reschly, 2007). This, in turn, allows students to focus more fully on their learning and feel more comfortable when asking questions and taking risks.

During this week, students should be finishing their group project from week three. Because they have an individual component to the project, students spend time working independently during this week. Students can rotate in and out of the various classroom structures, so this week often feels busy because students are continuously moving around, perhaps beginning the week with one partner and shifting to others for different aspects of the group assignment. As groups receive adequate time to confer, you can direct them back to work independently to complete their portion of the project. By the end of the week, this task should be complete and ready to present.

In week four, I recommend you avoid introducing new procedures because this is the week you want students to put together all the academic, behavioral, and social learning about your classroom. If you go back and review all the procedures you put in place, you have likely introduced your students to at least thirty procedures. The number of procedures should outweigh the number of rules inside of your classroom, as most behavior issues can be avoided using intentional procedures that focus on supporting relationships, a positive classroom environment, and a sense of belonging. According to Regina M. Oliver and Daniel J. Reschly (2007), rules serve the purpose of conveying clear and precise expectations for behavior using uncomplicated language and outlining consequences for any inappropriate conduct. If a student breaks a rule that does not require you to act immediately and give a consequence, you may need to revisit the rule to determine whether a procedure would be more appropriate.

Of course, establishing classroom procedures is not a one-time event. It is an ongoing process that requires regular reinforcement and revision. As the school year progresses, you may need to modify procedures or add new ones to accommodate changing circumstances. However, by establishing a strong foundation early on, you set your students up for success throughout the year.

How do you assess the overall impact of your classroom procedures and routines on student engagement, class participation, and overall academic performance?

_____

_____

_____

_____

_____

_____

_____

_____

_____

INTENTIONAL

MEANINGFUL

PRACTICAL

AUTHENTIC

CONSISTENT

TEAMWORK

> **Do you seek feedback from colleagues on your classroom procedures and routines? In what ways might you do that?**

_____

_____

_____

_____

_____

_____

_____

_____

_____

_____

Figure 5.1 offers a framework for planning your first twenty days of instruction.

Days	Structure	Procedures Taught	Purpose
1–5	Engage students as individuals.	• How to enter the classroom • How to begin morning work • How to go to the restroom • How to get additional supplies • How to submit classwork • What to do if they are tardy • How to exit the classroom • What to do if they have a question • Different discussion types	The purpose of this week is to teach students the necessary independent procedures they need in the classroom.

6–10	Group students in pairs to complete a task.	• How to transition into partner work • How to assign roles • How to submit assignments • How to transition back to individual places in the classroom • What to do if a partner is absent	During this week students are paired with someone in the classroom. Their partner may or may not remain the same. This week allows the teacher to see how students work together with one partner, observe personalities, and begin building student-student relationships.
11–15	Place students in small groups (about five students per group) with a group task to complete.	• How to transition into groups • How to gather needed supplies for everyone • How to assign roles within the group • What to do if someone is absent • What to do if someone does not contribute • How to submit group and individual assignments	This week focuses on how to move around the classroom when working on group tasks. Students are placed in a group for an entire week, allowing the teacher to observe how students behave in a group setting. Team-building activities are able to be embedded as students work in groups. Putting students who are familiar with each other into the same group allows teachers to observe students' responses and behavior.
16–20	Have student work in mixed structures, rotating between independent work, partner work, and group work, ending the week independently	The procedures from the previous weeks are reinforced and adjusted as needed based on how well they worked in the classroom.	Use this week to observe how well students are able to operate when using a variety of procedures in the classroom.

Figure 5.1: First twenty days of school framework.

*Visit **go.SolutionTree.com/SEL** for a free reproducible version of this figure.*

This framework can help you ensure you establish procedures and routines in the first weeks of school.

Closing Thoughts

Making a conscious effort to get to know your students and incorporate team-building activities in the first twenty days of school facilitates an intentional approach to teaching the necessary procedures and routines while fostering an inclusive classroom environment where every student feels valued. By taking great care in emphasizing how students should interact with one another during group work, regardless of their friendship status, a culture of mutual respect can be established between the teacher and students. "None of this happens by chance. It has to be carefully designed and implemented on a daily basis by the teacher" (Stafford-Brizard, 2024, p. 24). Each week of the first twenty days of school will provide you with the information needed to determine how your students fit into your classroom environment. Each week builds upon the next and allows you the chance to reflect on the classroom dynamics and adjust as needed. It is important you remain consistent in enforcing procedures that have been introduced, abandon those procedures that are not working, and incorporate additional procedures as needed. Your students' success depends on it, so stay the course and don't give up.

Chapter 5: Check Your IMPACT

1. How can I create opportunities to teach my students how to be successful in my classroom?

_____
_____
_____
_____
_____
_____
_____
_____

2. What are some proactive measures I can take to address potential disruptive behaviors?

_____
_____
_____
_____
_____
_____
_____
_____

3. How can I establish a culture of mutual respect between my students?

_____
_____
_____
_____
_____
_____
_____
_____

4. How can I foster an environment where students take ownership of their learning and manage their behavior?

_____
_____
_____
_____
_____
_____
_____
_____

5. How can I use team-building activities to foster an inclusive learning environment?

    _____

    _____

    _____

    _____

    _____

    _____

    _____

6. How often do I adjust my procedures and routines to accommodate the needs of my students?

    _____

    _____

    _____

    _____

    _____

    _____

    _____

7. Do I have more stated rules than procedures in my classroom?

    _____

    _____

    _____

    _____

    _____

    _____

    _____

8. How can I use the first twenty days of school to establish structure in my classroom?

    _____

    _____

    _____

    _____

    _____

    _____

    _____

9. How do I address noncompliance with classroom procedures and routines?

_____

_____

_____

_____

_____

_____

_____

10. How often do I review and reinforce classroom procedures and routines once they have been established?

_____

_____

_____

_____

_____

_____

_____

INTENTIONAL

MEANINGFUL

PRACTICAL

AUTHENTIC

CONSISTENT

TEAMWORK

Appreciate the Power of Teamwork

One of the joys of being a teacher is the relationships you form not only with your students, but also with your colleagues. The teacher-teacher relationship can help you get through the challenges inherent in being an educator.

I remember the year I transitioned from being a classroom teacher to a literacy coach. Not only was this my first school position outside of the classroom, but I was working with an entirely new staff. I had to figure out how to cultivate relationships with the teachers I was supporting, as well as the instructional coaching staff I would be working alongside. One thing that worked in my favor was I knew my content and was confident in my ability to transfer my knowledge into practice with adult learners. I possessed a sense of individual efficacy and was confident I could make an impact in my school community.

Even though my role changed from classroom teacher to literacy coach, I still took the same approach. I knew that a positive classroom environment, along with strong relationships, would be critical to our success as an ELA team. So, my first goal was to get to know my teachers. My first team meeting focused on who we were as people. I had the teachers complete an inventory form so I could learn their favorite treats, what a perfect day in the classroom meant to them, and how they like to be acknowledged. This inventory sheet was a powerful tool because it taught me so much about them and what motivated them.

During our meetings, I brought in some of their favorite treats for all to share so discussing data was not so daunting. I was also able to pair teachers based on their personalities and preferences so discussions would be productive and effective. This made the teachers feel as if they were being seen, heard, and acknowledged, so they were more open to the ideas, strategies, and interventions being implemented across the ELA team. Things ran efficiently. Teachers began to feel supported not only by me, but also by each other. We were able to discuss our content as a team and determine the instructional strategies and practices that would benefit all learners no matter the grade level. We also established the behavior expectations in the ELA classroom. Since the expectations were created as a team, teachers had a personal connection to them and enforced them with little to no pushback.

Because of our work as a team, we saw significant improvement in student behavior and achievement. We more than doubled our reading proficiency that year, and by the second year, we were a reward school for growth, which meant our students met and exceeded the achievement goal set by the state to ensure they were making adequate progress in the area of achievement. We would not have made such significant progress if we didn't come together as a team and work together. That was a true example of Teamwork Makes the Dream Work!

The sixth and final aspect of the IMPACT Framework is *teamwork*. This chapter will explore the importance of working with others to create safe spaces for learning, collaboration, and support. As an educator, your job is challenging enough—there is no need to try and operate alone when you and your colleagues are working toward the same goal of student success. Let's begin the chapter by discussing the importance of collective teacher efficacy. As you read through this chapter, consider how you can take advantage of the expertise and support of your colleagues.

Cultivating Collective Teacher Efficacy

With more demands being placed on teachers, getting to the business of educating your students may feel like an overwhelming challenge that should not be faced alone. To make true strides in improving the academic and social outcomes for your students, it's important to recognize the benefit of receiving support and encouragement from your colleagues. Although it's not a new concept, collective teacher efficacy (CTE) continues to be one of the strongest predictors of students' academic success. As highlighted by John Hattie in Visible Learning (n.d.), "Collective Teacher Efficacy (CTE) is the collective belief of teachers in their ability to positively affect their students." CTE has an effect size of 1.34, which is one of the most impactful actions educators can engage in (Visible Learning, n.d.). But to harness the power of CTE, teachers must be in an environment where they feel supported, valued, and heard.

As the teacher in your classroom, it is your responsibility to ensure that students are progressing academically and socially. However, your confidence in your individual ability to meet the needs of your students does not exclude the fact that teaching can be a demanding job, one that requires moral and professional support from other teachers who are experiencing similar challenges. The type of environment and culture needed to establish CTE is fueled by confidence, trust, and collaboration that develops as relationships develop among colleagues over time and through intentional efforts. In his article, "How Collective Teacher Efficacy Develops," Peter DeWitt (2019) describes CTE as the confidence that a group of teachers have in their collective ability to make a difference.

Not only does CTE help teachers improve their professional abilities, it can also bestow a sense of belonging within your school community. Just as our students look to be included in social networks among their peers, this is just as important to teachers. It would be difficult to address the social-emotional wellness needs of students if teachers felt they didn't belong to their own school community. "School members who have a strong sense of collective efficacy take on different roles to support the emotional state and value differences among each other, thereby decreasing the effects of stress, fear and anxiety by barriers" (Pierce, 2019). The cultivation of CTE not only improves academic outcomes for students, it also supports an environment in which teachers can thrive professionally and personally.

How can the cultivation of collective teacher efficacy improve your ability to perform professionally?

_____
_____
_____
_____
_____
_____
_____
_____
_____
_____

What are the barriers in achieving collective teacher efficacy, and how can they be addressed?

_____
_____
_____
_____
_____
_____
_____
_____
_____
_____

What steps can be taken among faculty and staff to ensure there is a culture of belonging among colleagues?

_____
_____
_____
_____
_____
_____
_____
_____
_____

INTENTIONAL

MEANINGFUL

PRACTICAL

AUTHENTIC

CONSISTENT

TEAMWORK

Find opportunities to collaborate. You may not always be able to plan as a grade-level team, but what about as a content team? This type of planning also offers you the chance to learn what skills the students in the same content area, but different grade levels, may need or lack based on their current year's instruction. So, don't discount the possibility of collaborating with peers even if you are not teaching the same grade level because you may discover additional teaching practices and strategies you wouldn't have otherwise. Brooke Stafford-Brizard (2024), Vice President of Innovation and Impact at the Carnegie Foundation, states, "Teachers need support from their peers and leaders to renew their capacity and development, which can be effectively addressed through creative and intentional approaches to scheduling and structures for collaboration" (p. 27). Just as students need to feel a sense of community to truly thrive, teachers are no different.

Following are some ways you can begin to foster the type of environment and culture that is conducive to supporting CTE.

▶ Design project-based learning (PBL) tasks as a multidisciplinary team in which all disciplines must be represented in the culminating task. This type of task requires collaboration and an examination of standards that relate to content areas. Each content teacher contributes their thoughts and ideas around their content and how it will enhance the overall learning experience. The culminating task should be presented to the school community since all content areas will be represented.

▶ Take time to get to know your colleagues by eating lunch together when the opportunity presents itself. Use this time as a chance to foster your relationship with colleagues and, as difficult as it may be, resist discussing your students.

▶ Promote schoolwide activities that allow teachers the opportunity to celebrate each other. Themed potlucks that a different grade level or content team sponsors each month are a great way to promote inclusivity. Teachers get to show off their favorite dishes while their colleagues get to enjoy a special treat.

▶ Participate in professional learning communities (PLCs) that allow all teachers across a school or district to share strategies and best

INTENTIONAL MEANINGFUL PRACTICAL AUTHENTIC CONSISTENT TEAMWORK

instructional practices with colleagues. In *Learning by Doing: A Handbook for Professional Learning Communities at Work* (DuFour et al., 2024), the authors state that a *PLC* is "an ongoing process in which educators work in recurring cycles of collective inquiry and action research to increase their learning and the learning of the students they serve" (p. 2). Committing to the PLC process allows teachers to gain additional knowledge and ideas from colleagues while making everyone feel like a valued member of their teaching community. It should be noted, though, that a PLC is not something individual teachers or even groups of teachers are empowered to create. It's a school- or districtwide effort that requires a guiding coalition to achieve, but this is part of what makes it a powerful collaborative process.

Collective Student Behavior Expectations

When you feel a genuine sense of belonging to your school community, you are better equipped to empathize with and address the social-emotional wellness needs of your students. Since a strong sense of CTE encourages teachers to use their professional strengths more effectively, teachers are more likely to address the social-emotional and academic needs of their students (Visible Learning, n.d.). Through this holistic approach to meeting the needs of students, teachers recognize that academic success is intertwined with students' social and emotional stability. When there is a culture of collective efficacy among teachers, students are more likely to feel seen, safe, and supported, knowing their teachers are not just concerned with their academic success but with their overall well-being:

> That is, whole child learning works because children and youth thrive in safe, supportive environments that create opportunities for students' social, emotional, and academic development. Children learn best when the content feels relevant to them and they feel a sense of purpose and agency in their work. (Rimm-Kaufman & Jodl, 2020)

A collaborative environment not only benefits students' academic success through the use of consistent instructional practices, it also benefits student behavior through the implementation of consistent discipline practices. These practices reinforce the expectations of behavior for all students from all teachers. A collaborative and collective approach should be developed through a shared vision of managing student behavior. This results in the use of practices and strategies that should be used consistently with your students so they can find value in them and feel safe in their school community and classroom (Shalaby, 2023).

How could you help your school community see the value in shared student behavior expectations?

_____

_____

_____

_____

_____

_____

_____

_____

_____

What are some barriers when developing team behavior expectations, and how can they be addressed?

_____

_____

_____

_____

_____

_____

_____

_____

_____

INTENTIONAL   MEANINGFUL   PRACTICAL   AUTHENTIC   CONSISTENT   **TEAMWORK**

Along the left margin (vertical text): INTENTIONAL · MEANINGFUL · PRACTICAL · AUTHENTIC · CONSISTENT · TEAMWORK

> **How might you address teammates who are not following through with shared team expectations? How can you ensure they feel valued when discussing team expectations?**

_____

_____

_____

_____

_____

_____

_____

_____

_____

_____

One of the ways you achieve a collective approach to managing student behavior is by ensuring all teachers share their expectations, understanding, and perspectives on how to approach and manage student behavior. The expectations for behavior should not be created in isolation, but they should be established through a collaborative and collective approach where all team members agree to adhere to and enforce them once they have been set. It is important that the behavior expectations are age-appropriate and are easily incorporated into the culture of your school.

Once the behavior expectations have been established, take time to ensure that students have been made aware of them. This step in the process is just as important as establishing the expectations as a team. You can't make assumptions that students will follow the expectations when they are set without being explicitly taught what they are and made aware of the consequences. It is the teacher's responsibility to manage classroom behaviors and expectations, and students can't be held accountable for expectations they didn't know existed. For any consequences to have the desired outcome, students must know which expectation they violated to understand why the consequence was given in the first place.

You can't rush past this step if you want full support from your administrators when it is necessary for them to deal with disruptive student behavior.

"Teachers have to do the legwork, so when they do need an administrator to step in, they can outline all the tools and strategies they have already tried so the administrator can understand why help is truly needed" (Bicknell, 2023, p. 59). So, if you want students to follow the expectations that have been set for their behavior, it is necessary for the team to take the time to ensure students know and understand what is expected of them in the classroom.

After behavior expectations have been established and taught to students with understanding, it is time to do the real work of enforcing them and following through with the consequence matrix that was created. This is where follow-through is most important and will require support from the administration in its initial stages. Your students will test the boundaries. This may cause discipline numbers to appear elevated in its initial stages, but as you and your teammates continue to enforce your expectations and adhere to the consequences, you will see the number of discipline issues level out. Students thrive in a positive classroom environment (Fisher, Frey, & Gonzalez, 2023) and will appreciate the structure and boundaries set for them to learn and feel safe in their classroom.

Figure 6.1 (page 136) shows an example of a planning template teams can use to create behavior standards and expectations for students. You can use this planning template throughout the school year and adjust it based on student behavior. As you are developing your behavior standards and expectations, bring any data available to justify the need for specific strategies and expectations. Some examples of data you can collect are classroom tardies, inappropriate restroom behavior, cellphone infractions, and general classroom disruptions. By bringing this information with you to the planning meeting, you and your teammates will be able to home in and focus on the most common disruptive behaviors. This will also allow you the chance to develop strategies specific to the behavior and determine if the strategies worked or not. Be sure to include administration in the planning process to ensure that consequences are appropriate and can be supported during the implementation of the plan because you will need administrative support. It will also be beneficial to communicate the expectations and consequences to parents so they are aware of student behavior expectations. Remember this is a collaborative and collective effort and should include as many stakeholders as possible to ensure effective implementation and success.

INTENTIONAL   MEANINGFUL   PRACTICAL   AUTHENTIC   CONSISTENT   TEAMWORK

INTENTIONAL MEANINGFUL PRACTICAL AUTHENTIC CONSISTENT TEAMWORK

Collaborative Behavior Management Plan: Classroom Transitions; Restroom Behavior		
Grade or Content Area: All-Grade-Level Plan		
Objective: To ensure classroom transitions run smoothly and minimize disruptive restroom behaviors and altercations		
Team Members:	**Date:**	**Meeting Agenda:**
	1/8/2025	• Discuss student behavior during hallway transitions. • Develop common transition procedures that all teachers can implement.
Behavioral Data:	**Strengths:**	**Challenges:**
• Office referrals from infractions during transitions • Altercations occurring in restrooms during transitions	• Most students follow outlined procedures regarding the restrooms during transitions • Teachers on their posts as directed	• Student tardiness • Behavior in restroom during transitions • Difficulty settling students after classroom transition
Behavior Expectations:	**Expectations Defined:**	**Alignment With School Expectations:**
• Students transition in allotted time • Students are not to be in the restrooms during transitions	• Bell schedule is visible • Hallway transition policy reviewed and explained in each class • Consequences for infractions during transitions explained	• Tardiness policy • Restroom policy during transitions • Schoolwide behavior expectations
Best Practice Strategies:	**Needed Adaptations:**	**Accommodations:**
• Explain classroom transition and restroom policies to student	• Students with special circumstance	• Permission for students with special circumstances • How are those circumstances decided?

• Allow questions and suggestions from students • Staff posted at restrooms to monitor		
Types of Data Collected:	**How Often:**	
• Referral data because of restroom infraction • Tardy slips for each class period	• Data will be reviewed every three weeks or more often if necessary	
Needed Supports:	**Needed Resources:**	**Needed Training:**
• Additional staff assigned to restrooms • Consequences given consistently	• Additional staff at restrooms	• None
Data Analysis:	**Artifacts Presented:**	**Modifications:**
• Review tardies to determine whether they declined • Review tardies to determine whether they occurred during specific class periods • Review ISS and OSS data to determine when/where behaviors occurred	• Tardy slips • Hall pass data	• Will be determined at next meeting based on student behavior in the restrooms and hallways during transitions
Action Plan:	**Additional Notes:**	**Next Meeting Date:**
• Get administration approval of team policy • Inform students and parents of new policy • Begin enforcing new policy • Begin collecting data	• Consequences need to be set • Determine date new policy goes into effect • Each teacher should keep all tardy slips given	• Three weeks

Figure 6.1: Behavior management plan template for class transition times.

Visit **go.SolutionTree.com/SEL** *for a free blank reproducible version of this figure.*

INTENTIONAL MEANINGFUL PRACTICAL AUTHENTIC CONSISTENT TEAMWORK

Collaborating to Address Students' SEL Needs

One of the key advantages of working as a team to support your students' social-emotional wellness needs is the heightened sense of recognizing shifts and changes within your student population. This comes as you and your team members work together, discussing behavior trends and sharing data (even if it is informal) that you may have collected surrounding particular behaviors. DuFour and colleagues (2024) find that education research has repeatedly linked school improvement to a collaborative culture. This research is significant because DuFour and colleagues (2024) could not find any additional research to refute the benefits of a collaborative culture and its effect on school improvement.

This collaboration does not stop with the improvement of academics. Through consistent collaboration that focuses on the issues surrounding students' academic and social-emotional wellness needs, teachers are better able to take a holistic approach when identifying strategies they can use within the classroom. Through regular analysis of student behavior, teacher teams are better able to make informed decisions while implementing practices that allow you to take a proactive stance in addressing the social-emotional wellness needs of students. This sharing of student behavior data also allows you to take a more targeted, data-driven approach when deciding how to tackle student behavior and needs.

How can a data-driven behavior approach help your team address students' SEL needs?

_____

_____

_____

_____

_____

_____

_____

_____

_____

_____

What ways can your team take a more collaborative approach when discussing and addressing students' SEL needs?

_____

_____

_____

_____

_____

_____

_____

_____

_____

What strategies have you used in your classroom practice that could benefit your team when addressing students' SEL needs?

_____

_____

_____

_____

_____

_____

_____

_____

_____

The best stance to take when addressing students' social-emotional well-being is a proactive one. Just when we think something won't happen, it does. At the end of the chapter, you'll find a reproducible reflection tool, "Teamwork SEL Practice" (page 144), that you can use with your team to practice addressing student social-emotional well-being.

INTENTIONAL

MEANINGFUL

PRACTICAL

AUTHENTIC

CONSISTENT

TEAMWORK

Closing Thoughts

One of the best ways to ward off unwanted behavior is to take a proactive approach and discuss behavior expectations beforehand. This ensures that you are not scrambling to implement expectations or interventions after situations arise. It would be beneficial to begin the school year by deciding as a team which behaviors are non-negotiable in everyone's classroom and will be given a standard consequence. This will help students understand that all teachers hold them accountable for their behavior. Then, try to streamline consequences for common behaviors that may happen periodically. This will provide some consistency in how students are penalized for inappropriate behaviors, as well as provide you and your teammates with the tools needed so you are not caught off guard when a consequence is necessary. To operate as a team, you must feel a part of the team. A genuine sense of belonging to your school community is crucial when it comes to empathizing and addressing your students' SEL needs. Where there is a culture of teamwork, students are more likely to feel seen, heard, and valued, knowing that all teachers are working towards their success.

INTENTIONAL

MEANINGFUL

PRACTICAL

AUTHENTIC

CONSISTENT

TEAMWORK

Chapter 6: Check Your IMPACT

1. How often do you and your team members share effective classroom management strategies?

_____

_____

_____

_____

_____

_____

_____

2. How often do you and your team members seek support from colleagues?

_____

_____

_____

_____

_____

_____

_____

3. Is support easily given and received from team members?

_____

_____

_____

_____

_____

_____

_____

4. In what ways could you further improve team communication and collaboration?

_____

_____

_____

_____

_____

_____

_____

5. How do you identify challenging behavior that needs to be addressed collectively?

_____

_____

_____

_____

_____

_____

_____

6. How well do you receive feedback from your team members?

_____

_____

_____

_____

_____

_____

7. How well do you align your team expectations with schoolwide expectations?

_____

_____

_____

_____

_____

_____

_____

8. How do you ensure your team efforts are in the best interest of the students?

_____

_____

_____

_____

_____

_____

_____

9. What types of data or evidence do you collect or use to justify your decisions around student behavior expectations?

_____

_____

_____

_____

_____

_____

10. How often do you communicate with parents about your team's expectations and the consequences of not adhering to them?

_____

_____

_____

_____

_____

_____

Teamwork SEL Practice

Read the following scenarios and answer the reflection questions that follow. After each scenario, take some time to discuss with your teammates how you would address the issues if they were to arise. You may have never experienced any of the scenarios, but it is good practice to think about how you would elicit the advice and support of your teammates if any of them were to happen.

Scenario One

Students have just returned from an extended break. Upon their return, you and your teammates begin to hear the chatter surrounding online bullying and arguments among a group of students. The students are in various classes, and the tension is mounting in the classrooms and during hallway transitions. Your team realizes that if something is not done to address these issues, you will lose control of student behavior.

1. How could you collaborate with your teaching team to identify the issues going on with your students?

_____

_____

_____

_____

_____

_____

_____

_____

_____

_____

_____

_____

_____

_____

_____

_____

_____

_____

_____

_____

2. You learn that the issues began because of something said online during an extended school break. What is your plan to address the issue?

_____

_____

_____

_____

_____

_____

_____

_____

_____

3. As a team, what support would you put in place for students who were affected by the cyberbullying?

_____

_____

_____

_____

_____

_____

_____

_____

_____

_____

4. How does your school handle cyberbullying? Are there any additional measures that can be put in place to ensure student safety?

_____

_____

_____

_____

_____

_____

_____

_____

_____

Scenario Two

During a Friday night football game, an altercation between two groups of students from different grade levels took place. It initially started as a war of words, but then a physical altercation occurred. School staff and security had to break up the fight, and the students were asked to leave the game. When students arrived at school on Monday, tensions were high, and you were told the students planned on finishing what they started on Friday during the school day, but you don't know when or where.

1. How would you and your team gather information about the initial altercation and the students involved without disrupting the classroom environment or instruction?

_____

_____

_____

_____

_____

_____

_____

_____

_____

_____

_____

_____

2. What interventions would you and your team put in place to ensure the safety of all students as you try to de-escalate the situation?

_____

_____

_____

_____

_____

_____

_____

_____

_____

_____

_____

_____

page 3 of 6

3. What steps would you take to try and de-escalate the tension between the two groups of students?

_____

_____

_____

_____

_____

_____

_____

_____

_____

_____

_____

4. How would you reinforce the schoolwide behavior expectations for all students?

_____

_____

_____

_____

_____

_____

_____

_____

_____

_____

5. How would you address the social-emotional well-being of students who were involved in the altercation?

_____

_____

_____

_____

_____

_____

_____

_____

_____

_____

_____

page 4 of 6

Scenario Three

A student in your class has experienced a significant loss recently and is overcome with grief. It is affecting their social-emotional well-being and their academic performance. You also notice the student's grief is beginning to affect their classmates and overall school environment.

1. How could you show support for the student without invading their privacy?

_____
_____
_____
_____
_____
_____
_____
_____
_____
_____
_____
_____
_____
_____

2. How would you approach the student while respecting their boundaries?

_____
_____
_____
_____
_____
_____
_____
_____
_____
_____
_____
_____
_____
_____

3. How do you support all students in this instance?

_____

_____

_____

_____

_____

_____

_____

_____

_____

_____

_____

_____

_____

_____

_____

_____

_____

_____

4. What safeguards could be put in place to address the classroom environment?

_____

_____

_____

_____

_____

_____

_____

_____

_____

_____

_____

_____

_____

_____

_____

_____

_____

_____

Epilogue

There is nothing like the joy of being an educator and seeing the impact you make in your students' lives. There will be moments in your career that you will never forget, and they will help you understand why you continue to show up day after day.

One of those moments for me was a special student award ceremony. All too often, the typical year-end awards ceremony consists of recognizing a few students from each classroom based on their academic performance—while the rest of the students sit and watch as the same students win over and over again.

That particular year, I wanted to recognize *all* my students, regardless of their grades in the gradebook. I wanted my students to imagine themselves as successful graduates, so I took pictures of each of my students wearing my graduation cap and gown while holding my college degree. They wrote a year-end essay that focused on how they saw themselves once they graduated from high school. Without the students knowing, I created a poster for each student and glued their photograph next to their essay, laminating each one so the students could keep it as a reminder of their dreams and aspirations at that time.

At the award ceremony, I surprised the class by calling up each student one by one to the podium to receive their own award. They were all so excited to be recognized and receive their pictures. Once I finished passing out all the "awards" I had my students take an oath of success. I'm not sure what happened to each of my students from that school year, but those I run into often remind me of that moment. They remember how special they felt to receive an award on that day, especially one that was specific to them. I also remember how *I* felt ensuring all of my students felt included—because I knew how it felt to feel ignored and as if I didn't matter.

This one moment represented the *impact* I wanted to make as a teacher.

▶ **Intentional:** I wanted to make sure all my students felt seen during that moment. Oftentimes, so many of our students feel invisible during those moments. Some of my students had never received a school award their entire school career, but I was able to change that in that moment.

▶ **Meaningful:** I gave my students a token of appreciation that meant something to them. It was beautiful to see my students stare at their poster, looking at themselves in the cap and gown holding that degree. I often wonder how it changed the trajectory of some of my students' lives being able to see themselves successful in school even if it was for a school project. The award ceremony was a moment for them to realize they could be anything they wanted to be.

▶ **Practical:** Let's be real. I was a teacher in the early 2000s. So, if we're discussing teacher pay now, imagine what it was like then. The most meaningful moments are sincere and genuine and don't require extravagant spending. Creating a keepsake that reminded students of their goals was a token that took time and effort to create, but my students truly appreciated the gesture.

▶ **Authentic:** It was authentic to who I was. I was never one that wanted to just single out a student here or a student there because they were the top performers. What about the students who never participated in class but had been trying their best for the last grading period? What about that student who struggled to write a proper sentence but pushed through and finished their essay? All of those students' efforts should be acknowledged because, for some of your students, that will be the only recognition they receive.

- ► **Consistent:** My behavior toward my students was very consistent. I quickly learned that I had to treat every day like a clean slate, and that included the awards ceremony. I remained consistent in how I treated my students, no matter what they said or did during class, or whether they complained about completing an assignment. I was determined to acknowledge my students and make each one of them feel special.

- ► **Teamwork:** Nothing I accomplished that year or the remainder of my time in the classroom was done alone. I had teammates who mentored me in my early years. I had teammates who supported me, and I had teammates who challenged me to increase my knowledge and capacity as an individual and educator. Being an educator is hard enough, so it is important to find your support system within your school community and beyond.

In what ways have you made an impact on the students you teach?

I hope you have enjoyed reading and working through my stories and the reflection activities in this book. I hope that my passion and love for education are apparent and have encouraged you to continue one more day in this challenging profession. One more day in fostering community in your classroom. One more day cultivating those relationships. One more day creating an environment that positively *impacts* your students' social-emotional wellness, so they can academically achieve their highest potential.

References and Resources

Aldrup, K., Carstensen, B., & Klusmann, U. (2022). Is empathy the key to effective teaching? A systematic review of its association with teacher-student interactions and student outcomes. *Educational Psychology Review, 34*(3), 1177–1216. https://doi.org/10.1007/s10648-021-09649-y

Armstrong, J. (2017, May 4). *Teaching students the power of vulnerability.* Accessed at https://mystudentvoices .com/teaching-students-the-power-of-vulnerability-531a593b11d1 on February 6, 2024.

Bailey, R., Stickle, L., Brion-Meisels, G., & Jones, S. M. (2019). Re-imagining social-emotional learning: Findings from a strategy-based approach. *Phi Delta Kappan, 100*(5), 53–58.

Barron, L., & Kinney, P. (2021). *We belong: 50 strategies to create community and revolutionize classroom management.* Arlington, VA: ASCD.

Battle, E. (2020, October 23). *My teachers couldn't understand my trauma, so I pledged to do better for my students* [Blog post]. Accessed at https://citizen.education/2020/10/23/my-teachers-couldnt -understand-my-trauma-so-i-pledged-to-do-better-for-my-students/ on April 10, 2024.

Bengtsson, H., & Arvidsson, Å. (2011). The impact of developing social perspective-taking skills on emotionality in middle and late childhood. *Social Development, 20*(2), 353–375.

Bicknell, K. (2023, November). To the teacher feeling unsupported with student behavior. *Educational Leadership, 81*(3), 58–63.

Brown, B. (2012). *Daring greatly: How the courage to be vulnerable transforms the way we live, love, parent, and lead.* New York: Gotham Books.

Buffum, A., Mattos, M., Malone, J., Cruz, L. F., Dimich, N., & Schuhl, S. (2024). *Taking action: A handbook for RTI at Work* (2nd ed.). Bloomington, IN: Solution Tree Press.

Center on Positive Behavior Intervention Supports. (2023, October 3). *Interconnected Systems Framework (ISF): Teaching and learning stories, a demonstration brief.* Eugene, OR: Author. Accessed at www.pbis.org /resource/interconnected-systems-framework-isf-teaching-and-learning-stories-a-demonstration-brief on February 6, 2024.

Chandler, G. A., & Budge, K. M. (2023). *Powerful student care: Honoring each learner as distinctive and irreplaceable.* Arlington, VA: ASCD.

Clarke, A., Sorgenfrei, M., Mulcahy, J., Davie, P., Friedrich, C., & McBride, T. (2021, July). *Adolescent mental health: A systematic review on the effectiveness of school-based interventions.* London: Early Intervention Foundation. Accessed at https://www.eif.org.uk/report/adolescent-mental-health-a-systematic-review-on -the-effectiveness-of-school-based-interventions on February 6, 2024.

Cobb, F., & Krownapple J. (2019). *Belonging through a culture of dignity: The keys to successful equity implementation.* Mimi & Todd Press.

Collaborative for Academic, Social, and Emotional Learning. (n.d.a). *Social and Emotional Learning (SEL) and student benefits: Implications for the safe schools/healthy students core elements.* Chicago: Author. Accessed at https://files.eric.ed.gov/fulltext/ED505369.pdf on February 6, 2024.

Collaborative for Academic, Social, and Emotional Learning. (n.d.b). *What is the CASEL framework?* Accessed at https://casel.org/fundamentals-of-sel/what-is-the-casel-framework/ on March 8, 2023.

Comer, J. P. (1995). Lecture given at Education Service Center, Region IV. Houston, TX.

Darling-Hammond, L., & Cook-Harvey, C. M. (2018, September). *Educating the whole child: Improving school climate to support student success.* Palo Alto, CA: Learning Policy Institute. Accessed at https:// learningpolicyinstitute.org/sites/default/files/product-files/Educating_Whole_Child_REPORT.pdf on February 6, 2024.

DeWitt, P. (2019, July). How collective teacher efficacy develops. *Educational Leadership, 76*(9). Accessed at www.ascd.org/el/articles/how-collective-teacher-efficacy-develops on February 6, 2024.

DuFour, R., DuFour, R., Eaker, R., Many, T. W., & Mattos, M. (2016). *Learning by doing: A handbook for Professional Learning Communities at Work* (3rd ed.). Bloomington, IN: Solution Tree Press.

DuFour, R., DuFour, R., Eaker, R., Many, T. W., Mattos, M., & Muhammad, A. (2024). *Learning by doing: A handbook for Professional Learning Communities at Work* (4th ed.). Bloomington, IN: Solution Tree Press.

Dyer, S. (2002). *Five little friends.* London: Bloomsbury.

Durlak, J. A., Weissberg, R. P., Dymnicki, A. B., Taylor, R. D., & Schellinger, K. B. (2011). The impact of enhancing students' social and emotional learning: A meta-analysis of school-based universal interventions. *Child Development, 82*(1), 405–432.

Egeberg, H. M., McConney, A., & Price, A. (2016). Classroom management and national professional standards for teachers: A review of the literature on theory and practice. *Australian Journal of Teacher Education, 41*(7), 1–18. https://doi.org/10.14221/ajte.2016v41n7.1

Ervin, S. (2022, December). Creating the safe and calm classroom. *Educational Leadership, 80*(4). Accessed at www.ascd.org/el/articles/creating-the-safe-and-calm-classroom on February 6, 2024.

Fisher, D., Frey, N., & Gonzalez, A. (2023, September). Four c's for better student engagement. *Educational Leadership, 81*(1). Accessed at https://ascd.org/el/articles/4-cs-for-better-student -engagement on February 6, 2024.

Fordham Institute. (2021, April 8). *Children learn best when they feel safe and valued.* Accessed at https:// fordhaminstitute.org/national/commentary/children-learn-best-when-they-feel-safe-and-valued on May 20, 2024.

Frey, N., Fisher, D., & Smith, D. (2019). *All learning is social and emotional: Helping students develop essential skills for the classroom and beyond.* Arlington, VA: ASCD.

Galla, C. K., & Goodwill, A. (2017). Talking story with vital voices: Making knowledge with Indigenous language. *Journal of Indigenous Wellbeing, 2*(3), Article 6.

Hattie, J. (2023). *Visible learning: The sequel—A synthesis of over 2,100 meta-analyses relating to achievement.* New York: Routledge.

Hayes, D., Mansfield, R., Mason, C., Santos, J., Moore, A., Boehnke, J., et al. (2023). The impact of universal, school based, interventions on help seeking in children and young people: A systematic literature review. *European Child & Adolescent Psychiatry*. https://doi.org/10.1007/s00787-022-02135-y

Hewlin, P. F. (2020, August 3). *How to be more authentic at work*. Accessed at https://greatergood .berkeley.edu/article/item/how_to_be_more_authentic_at_work on February 6, 2024.

Ho, J., & Funk, S. (2018). Promoting Young Children's Social and Emotional Health. *National Association for the Education of Young Children*, *73*(1). https://www.naeyc.org/resources/pubs/yc/mar2018/promoting -social-and-emotional-health

Hodges, H. (2001). Overcoming a pedagogy of poverty. In R. W. Cole (Ed.), *More strategies for educating everybody's children* (pp. 1–9). Arlington, VA: ASCD.

Hogenboom, M. (2019, October 1). *Why the way we talk to children really matters*. Accessed at https://www .bbc.com/future/article/20191001-the-word-gap-that-affects-how-your-babys-brain-grows on February 6, 2024.

Jones, S. M., & Bouffard, S. M. (2012). Social and emotional learning in schools: From programs to strategies and commentaries. *Social Policy Report*, *26*(4), 1–33. https://doi.org/10.1002/j.2379-3988.2012.tb00073.x

Jones, S. M., McGarrah, M. W., & Kahn, J. (2019). Social and emotional learning: A principled science of human development in context. *Educational Psychologist*, *54*(3), 129–143. https://doi.org/10.1080/00461520 .2019.1625776

Jones, S. M., Brush, K. E., Ramirez, T., Mao, Z. X., Marenus, M., Wettje, S., et al. (2021, July). *Navigating SEL from the inside out: Looking inside and across 33 leading SEL programs: A practical resource for schools and OST providers*. Cambridge, MA: Harvard Graduate School of Education. Accessed at https:// wallacefoundation.org/sites/default/files/2023-08/navigating-social-and-emotional-learning-from-the -inside-out-2ed.pdf on February 6, 2024.

Jung, L. A. (2023, November). Connection before correction. *Educational Leadership*, *81*(3). Accessed at https://www.ascd.org/el/articles/connection-before-correction on February 6, 2024.

Kafele, B. K. (2013). *Closing the attitude gap: How to fire up your students to strive for success*. Arlington, VA: ASCD.

LaBarbera, R. (2021, March 30). *How self-awareness enhances teaching*. Accessed at https://medium.com/age -of-awareness/how-self-awareness-enhances-teaching-a3f8b73d732 on February 6, 2024.

Lesley University. (n.d.). *5 ways to teach empathy and create "schools of belonging."* Accessed at https:// lesley.edu/article/5-ways-to-teach-empathy-and-create-schools-of-belonging on May 25, 2024.

Mason, V. L. (2021). *Teach up! Empowering educators through relationships, rigor, and relevance*. Boston: Houghton Mifflin Harcourt.

McKibben, S. (2022, November). Anindya Kundu on the difference between grit and agency (and why it matters). *Educational Leadership*, *80*(3), 14–18.

McKibben, S., & Smith, D. (2023, November). Following through on restorative practices. *Educational Leadership*, *81*(3). Accessed at www.ascd.org/el/articles/following-through-on -restorative-practice on June 22, 2024.

Mcleod, S. (2024, January 24). *Maslow's hierarchy of needs*. Accessed at www.simplypsychology.org/maslow .html on June 22, 2024.

Mikami, A. Y., Ruzek, E. A., Hafen, C. A., Gregory, A., & Allen, J. P. (2017). Perceptions of relatedness with classroom peers promote adolescents' behavioral engagement and achievement in secondary school. *Journal of Youth and Adolescence*, *46*(11), 2341–2354.

Minahan, J. (2023, November). A matter of perspective. *Educational Leadership*, *81*(3). Accessed at https://www.ascd.org/el/articles/a-matter-of-perspective on February 6, 2024.

National University. (n.d.). What is Social Emotional Learning (SEL): Why it matters [Blog post]. *National University*. Accessed at www.nu.edu/blog/social-emotional-learning-sel-why-it-matters-for-educators on March 27, 2023.

Nelson-Jones, R. (2014). *Practical counselling and helping skills: Text and activities for the lifeskills counselling model* (6th ed.). Thousand Oaks, CA: SAGE.

Nijhof, K., Te Brinke, L. W., Njardvik, U., & Liber, J. M. (2021). The role of perspective-taking and self-control in a preventive intervention targeting childhood disruptive behavior. *Research on Child and Adolescent Psychopathology*, *49*(5), 657–670.

Oliver, R. M., & Reschly, D. J. (2007, December). *Effective classroom management: Teacher preparation and professional development* [TQ Connection issue paper]. Washington, DC: National Comprehensive Center for Teacher Quality. Accessed at https://files.eric.ed.gov/fulltext/ED543769.pdf on February 6, 2024.

Osborne, J. (2021, January 27). *Managing classrooms with authenticity.* Accessed at https://medium.com/age-of-awareness/managing-classrooms-with-authenticity-f067d342e2f0 on February 6, 2024.

Osher, D. Kidron, Y., Brackett, M., Dymnicki, A., Jones, S., and Weissberg, R. (2016). *Advancing the science and practice of social and emotional learning: Looking back and moving forward.* Review of Research in Education, 40(1), 644-681.

Oxford Languages (n.d.). *Intentional.* Accessed at www.oed.com/search/dictionary/?scope=Entries&q=intentional on June 22, 2024.

Pierce, S. (2019). The importance of building collective teacher efficacy. *ACSA Leadership Magazine.* Accessed at https://leadership.acsa.org/building-teacher-efficacy on February 6, 2024.

Reibel, A. R. (2023). *Embracing relational teaching: How strong relationships promote student self-regulation and efficacy.* Bloomington, IN: Solution Tree Press.

Rimm-Kaufman, S. E., & Jodl, J. (2020, May). Educating the whole learner. *Educational Leadership*, *77*(8). Accessed at www.ascd.org/el/articles/educating-the-whole-learner on February 6, 2024.

Ruyle, M., Child, L., & Dome, N. (2022). *The school wellness wheel: A framework addressing trauma, culture, and mastery to raise student achievement.* Bloomington, IN: Marzano Resources.

Safir, S. (2023, April). Cultivating a pedagogy of student voice. *Educational Leadership*, *80*(7), 50–55. Accessed at www.ascd.org/el/articles/cultivating-a-pedagogy-of-student-voice on February 6, 2024.

Scheithauer, H., & Scheer, H. (2022). Developmentally appropriate prevention of behavioral and emotional problems, social-emotional learning, and developmentally appropriate practice for early childhood education and care: The Papilio approach from 0 to 9. *International Journal of Developmental Science*, *16*(3–4), 57–62.

Shalaby, C. (2023, September). Are we teaching care or control? *Educational Leadership*, *81*(1). Accessed at https://ascd.org/el/articles/are-we-teaching-care-or-control on February 6, 2024.

Souers, K. (2016). *Fostering resilient learners: Strategies for creating a trauma-sensitive classroom.* Arlington, VA: ASCD.

Stafford-Brizard, B. (2024, March). The power of educator EQ. *Educational Leadership*, *81*(6), 22–27. Accessed at www.ascd.org/el/articles/the-power-of-educator-eq on June 22, 2024.

Tomlinson, C. A. (2023, May). Teach up for equity and excellence. *Educational Leadership*, *80*(8). Accessed at www.ascd.org/el/articles/teach-up-for-equity-and-excellence on February 6, 2024.

Tyner, A. (2021, August). *How to sell SEL: Parents and the politics of Social-Emotional Learning.* Washington, DC: Thomas B. Fordham Institute. Accessed at https://fordhaminstitute.org/sites/default/files/publication/pdfs/20210811-how-sell-sel-parents-and-politics-social-emotional-learning826.pdf on February 6, 2024.

Viezzer, S. (2023, December 20). *Active listening: Definition, skills, and benefits.* Accessed at www.simplypsychology.org/active-listening-definition-skills-benefits.html# on February 6, 2024.

Visible Learning. (n.d.). *Hattie ranking: 252 influences and effect sizes related to student achievement.* Accessed at https://visible-learning.org/hattie-ranking-influences-effect-sizes-learning-achievement on February 6, 2024.

West Virginia Department of Education. (n.d.). *Behavior Interventionists.* Accessed at https://wvde.us/wp-content/uploads/2020/09/Behavior-Interventionists-One-Pager.pdf on June 8, 2024.

World Health Organization. (2021, November 17). *Mental health of adolescents.* Accessed at www.who.int//news-room/fact-sheets/detail/adolescent-mental-health/?gad_source=1&gclid=Cj0KCQiAwbitBhDIARIsABfFYILQ8PI36J2L1bsW2jMkYPgQptqoJcauNOLN8ZoxJ3hr5mafuC2mM0QaAmVQEALw_wcB on February 6, 2024.

Index

A Blueprint for Belonging
Morgane Michael

Equip educators with a toolbox of clear, concise, and practical strategies to foster a school culture of belonging and positivity. Author Morgane Michael empowers leaders and classroom teachers to construct a school environment that is welcoming and inclusive, providing a strong foundation for student social-emotional and academic success.
BKG185

Building Bonds With Learners
Patricia Erbe

Create more meaningful teaching experiences using the principles and methodology of the TSR model. Through research and experience, author Patricia Erbe provides a concrete plan educators can use to improve teacher-student relationships and promote better educational outcomes for their students.
BKG170

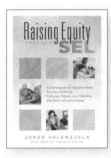

Raising Equity Through SEL
Jorge Valenzuela

How can you effectively address the academic and SEL needs of your diverse learners? By activating social-emotional learning within a framework that includes trauma-informed, culturally responsive, and restorative teaching practices.
BKG041

Embracing Relational Teaching
Anthony R. Reibel

Shifting from transactional to relational teaching empowers students and creates a more engaging classroom environment. This essential guide explores the why behind this shift and shares immediately applicable strategies for K–12 teachers.
BKF949